T0248117

Praise for *On the Origin of Christian Scripture*

David Trobisch is a signal figure in contemporary discussions of the Christian Bible's origins. What he makes clear in this expansive sketch of the various phenomena that produced the Bible's canonical edition is the interdependency of the *second* century's social world, the developing technology that produced collections of related writings, the literary marks and peculiar network of ecclesiastical figures that produced—perhaps inevitably so—the first editions of the church's biblical canon. Provocateur and poet, historian and hermeneut, Trobisch has drawn for us more a map than a monograph, and one that promises to guide future quests of an ancient history and help plot the tellings of this fascinating story of the Bible's real beginnings.

—**Rob Wall,** Seattle Pacific University

What is the Christian Bible, which books does it contain, and how, specifically, might one account for the formation of the New Testament? In his bold new book, *On the Origin of Christian Scripture*, David Trobisch engages these well-worn questions from a strikingly—and no doubt controversial—new perspective. Trobisch deftly articulates literary connections among what he thinks are several editorial interpolations throughout the New Testament, all of which shed light on the overall editorial purpose of the "Canonical Edition" of the New Testament. Bristling with fascinating and contentious insights, Trobisch's work will be sure to spark both conversation and intense debate. One thing is sure—his sweeping and unique synthesis of the New Testament canon cannot be ignored.

—**Darian Lockett,** Talbot School of
Theology, Biola University

With historical precision, Trobisch extends his innovative challenge to long-rehearsed theories about the formation of the New Testament canon, assembling further evidence for an early four-volume canonical edition of the Christian Scriptures.

—**Travis B. Williams,** Tusculum University

ON THE
ORIGIN OF
CHRISTIAN
SCRIPTURE

ON THE ORIGIN OF CHRISTIAN SCRIPTURE

The Evolution of the New Testament Canon in the Second Century

DAVID TROBISCH

Fortress Press
Minneapolis

ON THE ORIGIN OF CHRISTIAN SCRIPTURE
The Evolution of the New Testament Canon in the Second Century

Copyright © 2023 Fortress Press, an imprint of 1517 Media. All rights reserved. Except for
brief quotations in critical articles or reviews, no part of this book may be reproduced in any
manner without prior written permission from the publisher. Email copyright@1517.media or
write to Permissions, Fortress Press, 1517 Media, PO Box 1209, Minneapolis,
MN 55440-1209.

Library of Congress Control Number: 2023933504 (print)

Cover image: Four old books stacked ©PhotoMagicWorld / Alamy Stock Photo
Cover design: John Lucas

Print ISBN: 978-1-5064-8614-7
eBook ISBN: 978-1-5064-8615-4

Look at what is before your eyes, and you will
see what was hidden from you. (Jesus of Nazareth, Gospel of Thomas 5)

CONTENTS

I

THIS THING CALLED NEW TESTAMENT

HOW MANY BOOKS are included in the Christian Bible?

A Protestant Christian may say the Bible has sixty-six books, a Catholic may say seventy-three, a Greek Orthodox may say seventy-nine, and for an Ethiopian Orthodox Tewahedo Christian, eighty-one is the correct number of books in the Bible. And although from a scholarly point of view everyone who gives you a specific number is wrong, they give their answers with great conviction because the number was passed on to them with authority.

Fact is, there is no such thing as a Christian Bible. At least not if you define it by the number of writings it includes.

The four oldest physical copies of complete Christian Bibles are dated to the fourth and the fifth centuries. Like their modern counterparts, they consist of two parts, called the Old Testament and the New Testament. They differ in the number of Old Testament books, but in the New Testament part, they contain the same writings. So, one may say that there never was a clearly defined Old Testament, and one must say that there was and is a "Canonical Edition" of the New Testament. And if someone asks how many books are in the New Testament, there is a right answer: twenty-seven. If an edited collection has more or fewer than these twenty-seven writings, it is not a New Testament.

Few people will be surprised by the fact that the New Testament exists. At the same time, the implications of this insight are unsettling: someone must have selected and edited these writings for publication. The Canonical Edition of the New Testament, its design, and its origin are the topics of the following study.

But first things first.

The Distinction between Documents and Literature

In Egypt, the high culture and the dry climate have produced and preserved texts written on papyrus, the predecessor of modern paper. When something written on papyrus was discarded, it was thrown on a dump in the desert, away from the precious cultivated fields along the Nile River. The dry air of the desert preserved papyrus perfectly over the millennia. And it was on these African garbage dumps that the oldest fragments of the New Testament were discovered.

When a papyrus fragment is first assessed, a papyrologist makes a judgment as to whether the text is from a document or from literature. Although these terms have a much broader meaning in conversational language, papyrologists use them in a very specific way. A tax declaration, a receipt for goods received, a debtor's note, or a private letter are documents, just like a driver's license today or a diploma or a bank check or a receipt from a cash register is a document. A fragment that shows just a few words or sentences or pages from one of Homer's epics or Plato's discourses or Herodotus's *The Histories*, however, is designated by papyrologists as literature. Today's novels or memoirs or newspaper articles would also be called literature, not because of their artistic quality but simply because these texts are copied and disseminated in number. Literature only exists in copies; a document only exists in a single original. When a document is copied and the copies are disseminated, they become literature. In conversational language, we would probably call it publications and use the term *literature* to designate works of art. But papyrologists use the term in a more descriptive way.

Literary texts and documentary texts are distinguished by papyrologists because they require different methods of interpretation. Whereas every document is issued at a certain time and place by an identified issuer for a historically defined purpose, literature is designed to be useful for a variety of audiences, independent of geography, culture, and time. Documents can usually be dated very precisely and placed in a specific historical context. When it comes to literature, however, different people will find different observations meaningful.

There is no right or wrong, no universal significance that applies to everyone. No two readings of the same book will ever be the same, even by the same person. Published literature is an art form like performed music or paintings put on display to be viewed by the public. Lovers of music enjoy live concerts because repeated experiences of the same pieces are never identical. Literature, as art, refuses to be straightjacketed into one meaning.

The Distinction between History and Story

Aristotle, writing in the fourth century BCE, states that the work of a historian is so much easier than the work of a poet because the historian simply must state what happened, no matter if it sounds plausible to the reader or not. Facts are facts. The poet, however, does not write about what happened but about what he or she imagined may have happened or in the case of science fiction what he or she imagined may happen in the future.[1] The historian is not bothered if his audience does not believe him; he cannot but present the facts. The poet, however, must never lose the trust of his audience, or all his efforts will be in vain. The Greek term that Aristotle uses, πιστεύειν, modern translators of the New Testament translate as "having faith, believing."[2] A believer is someone who listens to a storyteller and believes him or her. The story that defines a faith community is the story about when, where, how, and why their faith community originated. If you do not believe it, you oust yourself. According to Aristotle, the successful poet turns his audience into a community of believers.

Most people easily distinguish between story and history in everyday life. Donald Duck, *The Lord of the Rings*, and *Star Wars* are stories. The events did not happen at the time and at the place where they happen in the narrative. And yet, we can relate to them, and we are willing to suspend our disbelief long enough to let us be drawn into the narrative world. When we read, we may meet people who have never lived, and still we connect and feel with them, are fearful or joyful, and we want to know what happens next.

Stories move from setting to setting, like the scenes of a stage play, with every setting providing a place in time and a specified location where characters interact. Conflicts move the plot through suspense and surprise, and as the drama evolves, these conflicts are tragically or comically resolved.

Real life rarely follows a script. But as we recount our own experiences, we try to please the people around us by turning history into a story. And the temptation to not let facts ruin a good story is often too strong to resist. Children learn early to cover up failures by lying about what happened because they cannot bear the disapproving reaction of their parent. It takes two to tango. And it takes an audience to turn history into story.

The result is that every story will contain historical facts. But it also may include imagined events that are communicated with plausibility. So, if the historian evaluates the account of a poet, he or she will have to look for independent confirmation because anything in a story could have happened or it could be a figment of the storyteller's imagination.

Scholars are called to differentiate between historical fact and imagined events. Distinguishing between story and history is a foundational pillar of the scholarly interpretation of biblical literature.

The Distinction between Historical and Implied Authors, Editors, and Publishers

Although Count Dracula, Frankenstein, Robinson Crusoe, Moby Dick, and Sherlock Holmes never existed, the authors who wrote about them, the editors who edited the manuscripts for publication, the publishers who sold the books, the millions of readers who bought and enjoyed the stories—they did and do exist. A story becomes history each time it is edited for publication and disseminated to be consumed. Publications are the incarnation of the spoken word.

The stories featuring Sherlock Holmes, for example, are written down by Dr. Watson. But because Dr. Watson is a character in the story, it is useful to use the term "implied author." The historical author is Arthur Conan Doyle.

The distinction between implied and historical is important to separate story from history. When authors, editors, or publishers are part of the editorial narrative, which is almost always the case with edited collections, they must not be confused with their historical counterparts. This distinction is of the utmost importance.

II

WHEN WAS THE CANONICAL EDITION FIRST PUBLISHED?

FOUR ANONYMOUS BOOKS about Jesus, twenty-one letters written by unknown persons to unknown people, rounded off with an anonymous book of stories and an anonymous book of revelations do not make for compelling reading. The authors' names mentioned in the title of each of the New Testament writings make a sizable difference.[1]

But how can we be so sure that Matthew or Mark or Luke or John had anything to do with the gospel books that are named after them? Why do some letters like "Letter of James" carry the name of the author in their title and others like "Letter to Romans" are named by those the letter addresses? How in the world could anyone call a letter "to Galatians," when Galatians depicts neither a city nor a person? And why is a "letter" to "Hebrews" usually printed among the letters of Paul, although the text does not mention the name Paul or use the term "Hebrews" anywhere?

Although the names of authors and titles are important, they are equally puzzles. Clearly, the selection of authors is intentional. And the genre designations as gospels, letters, acts, and revelation is helpful. So, who chose those names? Who formulated the titles? And when did this happen?

The following three chapters will address each of these questions. First, a look at the manuscript evidence confirms that the New Testament was carefully edited. Second, a survey of early documented readers gives us the backstory of the collection, which I call the "editorial narrative," that made the selection of writings meaningful to them. The third chapter presents sources outside the Canonical Edition that describe historical conflicts addressed in the editorial narrative. They give us an approximate date for the publication of the New Testament: the second half of the second century, more than a hundred years after Jesus's death.

§1
The Manuscripts of the New Testament

Before book printing was established in the sixteenth century, all texts were copied by hand. Roughly six thousand manuscripts, many of them mere fragments, with text of the New Testament survived the vagaries of time. Compared to other celebrated texts, like "The Odyssey," more copies, many more, of the New Testament survived. In fact, the New Testament is better attested than any other work of Greek literature.

The manuscript tradition of New Testament texts presents the Canonical Edition as a work of exactly twenty-seven writings organized into a collection of four volumes. Only one or two volumes were typically bound into a physical book, a *codex*. Less than 1 percent of all surviving manuscripts provide all four volumes bound together. And if they do, they do not always start with the four gospels or end with Revelation of John.

The Canonical Edition comprises the Four-Gospel volume, the Fourteen-Letters-of-Paul volume, the Acts-and-Catholic-Letters volume, and the Revelation-of-John volume. The writings within each of the four volumes are arranged in the same sequence and display uniform titles with few variants in the titles. Certain sacred terms like "God," "Lord," "Jesus," and "Christ" are contracted and marked with a line drawn above, the so-called *nomina sacra*.[2] The nomina sacra appear in the same form across all four volumes of the Canonical Edition of the New Testament.

The notation of *nomina sacra,* codex form, wording of the titles, uniform arrangement, and number of writings did not originate with the authors of the individual writings. Such literary phenomena were introduced by editors. Furthermore, it is unlikely that these elements can be the work of several editors operating independently and in isolation. More likely such consistent editorial interventions represent the work of a single editorial perspective. In other words, the Canonical Edition of the New Testament was edited and published by specific people, at a specific time, at a specific place, and for specific reasons.

Therefore, the shape of the New Testament is not random or even accidental; rather, the construction and arc of the New Testament demand that it be construed as a carefully edited collection. And like other edited collections, it expresses the message of the first publisher.

The question is, when did it reach this stable and fixed form, where, why, and by whom? It is possible that the individual books were copied for centuries before they became part of the edited collection. Forty years ago, the consensus of scholarship was that the New Testament grew over time, documents adhering to each other like individual barnacles on a pier, and was at some point, possibly under Emperor Constantine and as late as the fourth century, first prepared for publication.

Traditional studies from the nineteenth century relied heavily on interpreting statements from Christian authors in antiquity who were critical about the authenticity of certain writings—Letter to Hebrews, Revelation of John—or who never quoted from Second and Third Letter of John, Letter of Jude, and Second Letter of Peter, thus casting doubt on their authority and age. It is on this basis that scholars argued the Canonical Edition did not yet exist.

The evidence today is much better. In the twentieth century, manuscripts of the Canonical Edition were discovered, dated to the second and third centuries. These manuscript collections employ the codex at a time when literary works were still reproduced on scrolls. These collections feature *nomina sacra*. And if a fragmentary manuscript covers text from more than one writing and the sequence of these writings can still be recognized, because for example the page numbers survived, these writings are presented in the order found in the Canonical Edition.[3] And when a manuscript preserved a title, it is the editorial title used in the Canonical Edition—with very few exceptions.[4]

But early readers' skepticism about the authenticity of a specific writing hardly means that this writing was not yet part of their

Bible. In fact, quite the opposite. Only a reader who was familiar with Letter to Hebrews in a collection of Letters of Paul would have been prompted to discuss its authenticity. Discussions of authenticity do not necessarily prove that the Canonical Edition did not yet exist. To the contrary, it is more likely that these discussions by early readers confirm that the names in the titles of the Canonical Edition were understood as denoting historical authors.

Manuscripts, however, are notoriously difficult to date. The assessment as to whether a manuscript was produced in the second or third century is usually based on paleographical observations. Experts use skill and experience and compare the script to dated manuscripts, but in the end it is a judgment call and cannot be measured with an instrument. And experts are the first to confess that they can never be entirely sure that they got it right. Even if they got it right, a margin of twenty-five years up or down from their best call, accounting for the lifetime of the scribe, is as close as they can get. Scientific carbon dating, done by machines, analyzes the material the text is written on but not the ink. Writing on an old parchment at a much later time, for example, will skew the results. And the margin of interpretation is usually much higher than what paleographers suggest. The state of the scholarly consensus today, however, is that about sixty fragments have been dated by experts to the second and third centuries.[5]

Sometimes colleagues point out that one or more of these fragments could have come from an earlier edition than the Canonical Edition of the New Testament. Of course, this is possible, but not probable. When evidence is scarce, scholars must trade in probabilities. It is more probable that a fragment represents an edition attested for a much later period than to assume something that is otherwise not documented. It must be remembered that scholarly consensus is not about truth. It is about conclusions that can be communicated through interpreting evidence. Suspecting the existence of a publication that has left no other trace may be a correct assumption, but it will not hold up in the court of scholarly discourse. If fragmentary evidence fits a well-documented theory, this interpretation will win the day because, from a scholar's perspective, a theory that is based on ample evidence is to be preferred to a theory based on a single observation.

In conclusion, the consensus of scholarship assumes that the four oldest existing manuscripts that originally covered the entire New Testament were produced in the fourth and fifth centuries: Codex Sinaiticus, Codex Alexandrinus, Codex Vaticanus, and Codex Ephraemi Rescriptus.[6] Older fragmentary evidence of the Canonical Edition, reaching into the second and third centuries, exists and is compatible with the theory that the New Testament was published as an edited collection no later than the second century.

§2
Early Documented Readers

Four early Christian writers—Justin Martyr, Irenaeus of Lyons, Clement of Alexandria, and Tertullian of Carthage—corroborate a second-century date for the Canonical Edition of the New Testament. The writings of these "Church fathers" provide insight on how early readers might have understood the editorial narrative of the New Testament and how this narrative addressed specific historical circumstances during the middle to late second century.

Justin Martyr of Rome (*First Apology,* ca. 155–157)

Justin Martyr, writing in Rome for a non-Christian audience, explained that the apostles composed memoirs that his faith community called gospels.[7]

> *For the* apostles, in the memoirs composed by them, *which are called* Gospels, *have thus delivered unto us what was enjoined upon them. (Apology I, 66)*

Justin speaks about several gospels, not just one, and states that they were written by apostles. They were not anonymous.

The titles of the New Testament writings are an editorial feature of the Canonical Edition. The editors name the four books about Jesus "gospels." In regular usage, the Greek term for "gospel" means "good news" and refers to a message, not to the genre of a book. But because the editors of the Canonical Edition used the term in the titles of four different writings, the term becomes a genre description; it describes the constellation of literary properties these four books share. The observation that "gospel" is not used in book titles outside of Christian publications is confirmed by Justin, who feels obliged to explain to his audience that the books "called gospels" are like "memoirs." Justin is here relating the unknown genre, gospel, to an already-known genre, memoir. The editors of the Canonical Edition add "according to" in the title of their four gospel books and associate each writing with a name: Gospels according to Matthew, Mark, Luke, and John. We cannot be certain that Justin refers to the Canonical Edition of the New Testament, but his description coheres with the Four-Gospel volume nicely.

Justin further explains that texts from these gospels were read aloud during Sunday services together with the "writings of the prophets" and that a sermon followed.

> *And on the day called Sunday, all who live in cities or in the country gather together to one place, and the* memoirs of the apostles *or the* writings of the prophets *are read, as long as time permits; then, when the reader has ceased, the president verbally instructs, and exhorts to the imitation of these good things. (Apology I, 67)*

The Christian Bible is structured in two parts, the "Old Testament" and the Canonical Edition of the "New Testament." A shared theme of most New Testament writings is that the prophetic writings of Israel and Judah foreshadow the coming of Jesus the Christ. Justin's witness that "writings of the prophets" are read aloud to congregations alongside the "memoirs of the apostles" fits the message of the Canonical Edition.

Not all Christians, however, agreed with this interpretation of the prophets. In the immediate context, Justin singles out the Marcionite faith community. "They laugh at us," Justin writes.

And, as we said before, the devils put forward Marcion of Pontus, who is even now teaching men to deny that God is the maker of all things in heaven and on earth, and that the Christ predicted by the prophets is His Son, and preaches another god besides the Creator of all, and likewise another son. And this man many have believed, as if he alone knew the truth, and laugh at us, though they have no proof of what they say, but are carried away irrationally as lambs by a wolf, and become the prey of atheistical doctrines, and of devils. (Apology I, 58)

According to Justin, the Marcionite community assumed that the creator of the material world was not the father of Jesus. The divine Father of Jesus was much higher up in the hierarchy of gods than the creator god.

Justin registers the diversity of the Christian movement by clarifying that the Marcionite community are "called Christians" as well.

And there is Marcion, a man of Pontus, who is even at this day alive, and teaching his disciples to believe in some other god greater than the Creator. And he, by the aid of the devils, has caused many of every nation to speak blasphemies, and to deny that God is the maker of this universe, and to assert that some other being, greater than He, has done greater works. All who take their opinions from these men, are, as we before said, called Christians. (Apology I, 26)

The debate was about whether God created the world with all its imperfections or whether "the aid of devils" is to be blamed for the sinful character of humans, as Justin in his damning judgment of Marcion assumes.

Irenaeus of Lyons (*Against Heresies*, ca. 180)

Irenaeus of Lyons, modern-day France, published his five-volume work, *On the Detection and Overthrow of the So-Called Gnosis*, about two decades after Justin. This book is usually referred to as *Against Heresies*.[8]

As he refutes a certain Valentinus, who was the author of a book called the *Gospel of Truth*, Irenaeus argues that only four gospel books serve as pillars of the Church.

> *It is not possible that the Gospels can be either more or fewer in number than they are. For, since there are four zones of the world in which we live, and four principal winds, while the Church is scattered throughout all the world, and the "pillar and ground" of the Church is the Gospel and the spirit of life; it is fitting that she should have four pillars, breathing out immortality on every side, and vivifying men afresh. (*Against Heresies 3:11:8)*

Because the four authors Matthew, Mark, Luke, and John appear in the exact order as they do in the Four-Gospel volume, Irenaeus is most likely depending on the Canonical Edition. The likelihood increases because he also testifies to the existence of competing publications. Irenaeus serves as a valuable source to document how an early reader of the Canonical Edition understood its editorial narrative in contrast to rival publications.[9]

> *For, after our Lord rose from the dead, [the apostles] were invested with power from on high when the Holy Spirit came down [upon them], were filled from all [His gifts], and had perfect knowledge: they departed to the ends of the earth, preaching the glad tidings of the good things [sent] from God to us, and proclaiming the peace of heaven to men, who indeed do all equally and individually possess the Gospel of God. Matthew also issued a written Gospel* among

> the Hebrews in their own dialect, *while Peter and Paul were preaching* at Rome, *and* laying the foundations of the Church. *After their departure,* Mark, *the disciple and interpreter of Peter, did also hand down to us in writing what had been preached by Peter.* Luke *also, the companion of Paul, recorded in a book the Gospel preached by him. Afterward,* John, *the disciple of the Lord, who also had leaned upon His breast, did himself publish a Gospel during his residence at Ephesus in Asia. (Irenaeus,* Against Heresies *3:1:1; cf. Eusebius,* Ecclesiastical History *5:8:2–4)*

After Jesus was resurrected and the apostles received complete knowledge and the power of the Holy Spirit, they traveled to the ends of the earth and proclaimed God's message. Matthew wrote his book in Hebrew, while Peter and Paul "laid the foundations of the Church" in Rome. Mark recorded Peter's message and Luke recorded Paul's message. The Beloved Disciple John published his account in Ephesus after the other three gospel books were finished.

The story of origins provided by Irenaeus stands in contrast to the one taught in most universities worldwide. To pass their exams, university students must learn and rehearse something like this:

The oldest book in the New Testament is Paul's First Letter to Thessalonians. The other authentic letters of Paul are Romans, 1 and 2 Corinthians, Galatians, Philippians, and Philemon. These letters were penned and delivered during the two decades after Jesus's death, but the exact dates and ordering are obscure. All other books were probably *not* written by the authors suggested in the titles.

Hebrews was not written by Paul; 1 and 2 Timothy and Titus, the so-called Pastoral letters, were added to the authentic letters of Paul in the second century, and the authenticity of Colossians, 2 Thessalonians, and Ephesians remain disputed. None of the Catholic Letters—James; 1 and 2 Peter; 1, 2, and 3 John; and Jude—are authentic. The author of Revelation is unclear; several candidates named John were discussed as early as the second century. When it comes to the gospels, the gospel book attributed to Mark was written first, before 70 CE, mainly because it does not seem to reflect the fall of Jerusalem and the temple. The anonymous writers or editors who put Luke and Matthew together used Mark and shared another written account that is now lost, the source called Q (a source reflected in the overlaps between Matthew and Luke not found in Mark). Matthew and Luke were composed after the fall of Jerusalem. In addition to Mark and Q, so the story goes, Matthew and Luke relied on information of unidentified origin, possibly oral traditions. The relationship between John and the other three gospel books is highly problematic, leaving the scholarly community locked in a battle as to whether the unidentified author of John's gospel book knew the three Synoptic Gospels or not.

At an unspecified point in history, the church decided what to accept into the canon and what to exclude from it.

Clearly, the historical narrative about how the New Testament was put together is quite different from Irenaeus's story. Whereas historians look at the single writings as documents, Irenaeus looks at their collection as literature. The editorial narrative of an edited collection is a story; historical assessments, however, accept information only if it can be verified by evidence independent of the literature under scrutiny. The difference is striking.

In his portrayal of Marcion, Irenaeus agrees with Justin. Marcion "taught that the God proclaimed by the law and the prophets was not the Father of our Lord Jesus Christ."[10] Marcion published an edited collection that consisted of one gospel book and ten letters of Paul. Irenaeus thinks that the gospel book was a strongly redacted version of Gospel according to Luke and that the letters were an abridged edition of the Fourteen-Letters-of-Paul volume of the Canonical Edition.

> *Besides this, he mutilates the Gospel which is according to Luke,*
> *removing all that is written respecting the generation of the*
> *Lord, and setting aside a great deal of the teaching of the Lord,*

*in which the Lord is recorded as most dearly confessing that the
Maker of this universe is His Father. . . . In like manner, too,
he dismembered the Epistles of Paul, removing all that is said
by the apostle respecting that God who made the world, to the
effect that He is the Father of our Lord Jesus Christ, and also
those passages from the prophetical writings which the apostle
quotes, in order to teach us that they announced beforehand the
coming of the Lord. (*Against Heresies *1:27:2)

Although the Marcionite Edition is well attested and extensively quoted
by its detractors, no manuscripts survived. Scholars have pointed out
that the title of the Marcionite Edition probably was "New Testament," and that the gospel book was simply called "Gospel" with no
attribution to its author.[11]

Clement of Alexandria (*Stromata,* ca. 200–215)

Clement of Alexandria (Egypt), who wrote his books about two decades
after Irenaeus, uses the terms *Old* and *New Testament* for the two parts
of the Christian Bible. He quoted from the Canonical Edition of the
New Testament more than thirty-two hundred times.[12]

In his apologetic efforts, Clement used the "argument of age"
(the oldest is to be preferred), an argument that was often repeated in
the history of interpretation and still is widely used today, to defend
the credibility of the Canonical Edition. He understood the editorial
narrative the same way Justin and Irenaeus did: the New Testament
only contained authentic writings from the first century, and therefore
it was older than the editions produced by recent heretics.

*For that the human assemblies which they [= the heretics]
held were posterior to the Catholic Church requires not many
words to show. For the teaching of our Lord at His advent,
beginning with Augustus and Tiberius, was completed in
the middle of the times of Tiberius. And that of the apostles,*

> *embracing the ministry of Paul, ends with Nero. (Clement,*
> Stromata *7:17)*

Clement assumes that Jesus was born under Emperor Augustus because Gospel according to Luke presents it that way.[13] He states that Paul died during the reign of Nero because Acts of Apostles references Claudius, Nero's predecessor, during the time that Paul was arrested and brought to Rome.[14] Clement assumes that the era of the apostles who wrote the books of the Canonical Edition came to an end under Emperor Nero. Historically, Nero committed suicide on June 9, 68 CE.

> *It was later, in the times of Adrian the king, that those who invented the heresies arose; and they extended to the age of Antoninus the elder, as, for instance,* Basilides, *though he claims (as they boast) for his master, Glaucias, the interpreter of Peter. Likewise they allege that Valentinus was a hearer of Theudas. And he was the pupil of Paul. For* Marcion, *who arose in the same age with them, lived as an old man with the [heretics]. And after him Simon heard for a little the preaching of Peter. (*Stromata *7:17)*

Books about Jesus by heretics like Basilides and Marcion were published more than a century after Jesus's death. Emperor Hadrian ruled from 117 to 138 CE and was succeeded by Emperor Antoninus, who died 161 CE. The argument of age encourages readers to put their trust in first-century writings.

> *Such being the case, it is evident, from the high antiquity and perfect truth of the Church, that these later heresies, and those yet subsequent to them in time, were new inventions falsified [from the truth]. (*Stromata *7:17)*

Like Irenaeus, Clement of Alexandria linked the Canonical Edition to the "truth of the Church."[15] The statement also reflects a dismissive perception toward second-century books on Jesus and his apostles; they were expected to be fictional.

> *We say that* the old and catholic church . . . *gathered those into the one faith who were predestined by God to be righteous. Their faith is* according to their own Testaments. . . . *One Testament was* given through God's *will at different times than the other one, which was* given through the Lord. (Stromata 7:17)

The "old and catholic church," as Clement calls the faith community with whom he identifies, organizes congregations of those who God will save, and their faith is based on a specific edition. The expression "according to their *own* Testaments" referenced the title of the Christian Bible, New and Old Testaments, and characterized the edition as something that the church "owned," that belonged to one's house or family.[16] The Old Testament was given through "God's will"; the New Testament was given through the "Lord" Jesus the Christ. In other words, whoever did not accept the truth expressed in this edition was not part of the family, not brothers and sisters in faith.

The links between text and faith, edition and truth, are established by Clement of Alexandria. Although the Marcionite faith community believed in Jesus as the Christ, they were heretics because they did not use the Canonical Edition of the New Testament.[17]

Tertullian of Carthage (*Adversus Marcionem,* ca. 208)

Irenaeus was hoping to refute Marcion's teaching using the Marcionite Edition, but never did.[18] A few decades after Irenaeus, however, Tertullian of Carthage, in modern-day Tunisia, North Africa, picked up the idea and published a five-volume work, *Against Marcion*, in which he quoted the Marcionite Edition of the New Testament extensively. By doing so, he left the most complete record and description of this lost work.

Recent scholarship supports the theory that the Marcionite community had not created the Marcionite Edition, they only used it.[19] The argument rests upon the observation that the edition does not support Marcion's theology and that it was used by Christian groups unrelated to the Marcionite movement. Tertullian's association of the gospel book with Marcion, however, stuck in the history of interpretation. To make the discourse with traditional research not too awkward and unwieldy, I refer to this edited collection, which comprised one gospel book, ten letters of Paul, and possibly carried the title "New Testament," as the *Marcionite Edition of the New Testament*.

Tertullian, however, repeats the messaging of his precursors: he was convinced that Marcion had redacted the Canonical Edition, and he reiterated that Marcion believed that the god who created the material world according to Jewish Scriptures was a different supernatural power than the God of Jesus.

> *What Pontic mouse ever had such gnawing powers as he who has gnawed the Gospels to pieces? . . . The heretic of Pontus introduces two Gods, like the twin Symplegades of his own shipwreck: One whom it was impossible to deny, i.e. our Creator; and one whom he will never be able to prove, i.e. his own god. (Tertullian,* Against Marcion *1:1–2)*

Like Clement of Alexandria, Tertullian endorsed the argument of age. His refutation of Marcion was simple: Whoever had the older version had the original.

> *I affirm that Marcion's Gospel is adulterated; Marcion, that mine is. Now what is to settle the point for us, except it be that principle of time, which rules that the authority lies with that which shall be found to be more ancient. (*Against Marcion *4:4)*

Tertullian's intellectual error, shared with Justin, Clement of Alexandria, and Irenaeus, was that they took the editorial narrative of the

Canonical Edition, which ascribed all writings of the New Testament to eight authors of the first century, for reliable historical information. They failed to distinguish between story and history.

Tertullian and his peers may have committed another grave mistake. Because the Marcionite faith community used a specific edition, he assumed that it had been created by its founder, Marcion. This is not a necessary conclusion.

Just because Mormons use the King James Version of the Christian Bible does not mean that Joseph Smith, the founder of the Church of Jesus Christ of Latter-day Saints, created it. The Marcionite Edition of the New Testament certainly did not support the concept of a lesser god who created the world and who stood in competition with a higher-ranking god, the Father of Jesus. Tertullian's view that Marcion and his associates put the gospel book and ten letters of Paul together to support their theology is untenable.

When the Marcionite Edition is viewed as literature, there can be little doubt that the gospel book was associated with Paul. Readers of the collection have no other character to choose from. This gospel book is only "anonymous" when the literary context is ignored. In the introduction to the first letter of the Marcionite Edition, the letter to Galatians, Paul writes: "Even if we or an angel from heaven should proclaim to you a gospel contrary to what we proclaimed to you, let that one be accursed!" (Galatians 1:8). Paul endorses the gospel book that stood next to Paul's letters in this edition.

§3
Provenance, Historical Conflict, and the Canonical Edition

Early documented readers share a narrative about who authored the writings of the Canonical Edition and when: They were written by eight authors between the time of Jesus's death and Paul's death. These books were arranged in four volumes and published under the title New Testament.

In the world of manuscripts and museums, a rare book with a provenance record is worth a lot more than a copy of the same edition without a documented history of ownership. In the art trade, provenance records are essential to unmask fraudulent activity. Provenance, in this context, refers to the documented chain of owners and custodians of an artifact. Provenance certifications are based on documents like receipts of financial transactions, proof of public exhibits, dated photographs of the item, letters of past scholarly appraisals, library acquisition papers, itemized tax declarations, and insurance payments. But sometimes, only an affidavit is available, a so-called provenance letter. It is usually handwritten by the owner of the artifact and notarized. The letter might state, for example, that a certain rare book was in the possession of the family for centuries and had been passed on from generation to generation, explaining why there are no previous records of its existence. Most seasoned collectors will have a story, how, at a flea-market or a garage sale or in a shed or under the roof of someone's home, they discovered something precious. Stories of miraculous discoveries often want to explain the lack of documented provenance, and the motivation behind such narratives is often the desire to create public interest. A provenance narrative may or may not describe historical facts.

Collectors know what they are looking for. Many of them enjoy the hunt more than owning a rare item. Some collectors will proudly sell the item, touting how much money they received, or they may donate it to a reputable institution that will honor the collector's effort in perpetuity by accepting it into the institution's collection and occasionally putting it on display. Other collectors treasure their precious finds—like the merchant in Jesus's story who sold everything he owned to acquire a special pearl. Auction catalogues, dealer descriptions, and exhibition labels in museums like to use superlatives—*the oldest, the most recent, long-lost, for the first time on display*—sometimes suggesting that "history has to be rewritten!" This is what collectors love to claim and the public desires to hear.

It's no wonder, then, that provenance letters are sometimes fabricated, and matters confused. The item may indeed be old and genuine, but the document proving the history of ownership may be fictitious and misleading. Scholarly experts concentrate on descriptions of the genuine artifact, while legal advisors may only want to make sure that a provenance record exists. It is easy to become disillusioned and skeptical of the art trade. Provenance letters with stories of a miraculous discovery satisfy the dreams of trusting souls who want to believe what sounds too good to be true. A compelling story will often go a long way to cover up the lack of documentary evidence.

Irenaeus published a provenance narrative for the Canonical Edition of the New Testament. What is to be made of his narrative?

Irenaeus's Provenance Narrative

Irenaeus assumed that the New Testament faithfully preserved first-century documents unaltered. According to Irenaeus, the chain of custody began with bishop Linus of Rome, who is mentioned in Second Letter to Timothy.[20]

> *The blessed apostles, then, having founded and built up*
> *the Church, committed into the hands of Linus the office*
> *of the episcopate. Of this Linus, Paul makes mention in*
> *the Epistles to Timothy. To him succeeded Anacletus; and*
> *after him, in the third place from the apostles, Clement was*
> *allotted the bishopric. . . . To this Clement there succeeded*
> *Evaristus. Alexander followed Evaristus; then, sixth from*
> *the apostles, Sixtus was appointed; after him, Telesphorus,*
> *who was gloriously martyred; then Hyginus; after him, Pius;*
> *then after him,* Anicetus. *Soter having succeeded Anicetus,*
> Eleutherius *does now, in the twelfth place from the apostles,*
> *hold the inheritance of the episcopate. In this order, and by*
> *this succession,* the ecclesiastical tradition from the apostles,
> and the preaching of the truth, *have come down to us. And*

> *this is most abundant proof that there is one and the same*
> *vivifying faith, which has been* preserved in the Church
> from the apostles until now and handed down in truth.
> *(Irenaeus,* Against Heresies *3:3:3)*

Although the list of bishops was brought all the way from Paul and the apostles to Eleutherius, who was the Bishop of Rome at the time Irenaeus was writing his book, Irenaeus was mainly interested in showing the succession from Paul to Anicetus. The chain of custodians sets the stage for his report of the historic meeting between Anicetus of Rome and Polycarp of Smyrna that follows in the narrative.

> *But* Polycarp *also was not only* instructed by apostles, *and*
> *conversed with many who had seen Christ, but was also,*
> by apostles in Asia, appointed bishop of the Church in
> Smyrna, *whom I also saw in my early youth, for he tarried*
> *[on earth] a very long time, and, when a very old man,*
> *gloriously and most nobly suffering martyrdom, departed this*
> *life, having always taught the things which he had learned*
> *from the apostles, and* which the Church has handed down,
> *and which* alone are true. *(Irenaeus,* Against Heresies *3:3:4)*

Irenaeus highlights that Polycarp was instructed by apostles and appointed as Bishop of Smyrna, which makes Polycarp a custodian of the apostolic tradition and gives him the same credentials as Anicetus. Keeping in mind that Irenaeus began this section by endorsing the four canonical Gospels through the authority of the apostles who "indeed do all equally and individually possess the Gospel of God" (Irenaeus, Against Heresies 3:1:1), the argument has now returned to its main theme, the endorsement of New Testament writings as literary products of the first century.

> *He it was who, coming to Rome in the time of Anicetus caused*
> *many to turn away from the aforesaid heretics to the Church*

of God, proclaiming that he had received this one and sole truth from the apostles, *—that, namely, which is* handed down by the Church. *(Irenaeus,* Against Heresies *3:3:4)*

The instructions of the apostles have been "handed down" by "the Church," and they "alone are true." Anicetus of Rome together with Polycarp of Smyrna guarantee the authenticity of these writings, and their transmission.

A Historical Conflict

Scholars have pointed to political conflicts as historical triggers for the publication of edited collections. The Pseudo-Isidorian Decretals, for example, were collected, edited, and published to be introduced in a trial in the ninth century.[21] The enlarged and revised edition of the Letters of Ignatius, which dominates the manuscript tradition, addressed the Arian Controversy, and was put together by a certain Julian between 350 and 380.[22] Duke Rudolph IV published a collection of documents when the influence of his family on the election of the Emperor of the Holy Roman Empire was in jeopardy in the fourteenth century.[23]

During the second century, the Canonical Edition clashed with the Marcionite Edition, as both include some of the very same material and pitted two faith communities against one another. According to the editorial narrative of the Marcionite Edition, Paul himself had edited "The Gospel" and ten of his letters for publication.[24] According to Irenaeus, Polycarp declared that unbeknownst to the public, an exemplar of the gospel book that was older than Marcion's gospel had been kept in church archives in Asia Minor for more than a century, together with a more complete collection of Paul's letters. Such a claim would have found open ears in Rome because, according to Tertullian, Marcion had been excommunicated from the Roman congregation about one or two decades before Polycarp visited.[25] And because Polycarp spoke as the representative of the Catholic bishops in Asia Minor, the region from which Marcion and other heretics came,

Anicetus almost certainly would have been inclined to endorse such a discovery.[26]

Irenaeus's support of Bishop Polycarp of Smyrna reflected that sentiment. In the eyes of Irenaeus, Polycarp authenticated the Canonical Edition for his Roman audience and exposed the Marcionite Edition as a fraud.

A second conflict, reflected in the decision to publish a Canonical Edition, is the so-called *Easter Controversy*, which is also well documented outside of biblical literature. In a letter to Victor, the Bishop of Rome, which is preserved in Eusebius's Ecclesiastical History, Irenaeus brings up Polycarp's visit in a different context.

> *And when the blessed Polycarp was at Rome in the time of Anicetus, and* they disagreed a little *about certain other things, they immediately made peace with one another, not caring to quarrel over this matter. For neither could Anicetus persuade Polycarp not to observe what he had always observed with* John the disciple of our Lord, *and the other apostles with whom he had associated; neither could Polycarp persuade Anicetus to observe it as he said that he ought to follow the* customs of the presbyters *that had preceded him.*
>
> *But though matters were in this shape, they communed together, and* Anicetus conceded the administration of the eucharist in the church to Polycarp, *manifestly as a mark of respect. And they parted from each other in peace, both those who observed, and those who did not, maintaining the peace of the whole church. (Eusebius,* Ecclesiastical History 5:24:16–17)

Eusebius uses Irenaeus's letter to illustrate a dispute over when to commemorate Jesus's crucifixion in the ecclesiastical calendar. Churches in Asia Minor observed Jesus's death in the afternoon of the day of the Jewish Passover. This tradition also assumed that Jesus was resurrected the same day he was crucified and, therefore, the period of fasting should end on the day of Passover, which could potentially fall on any day of the week. The Roman Christian community, however, would first determine the date of Easter Sunday as the first Sunday after the first full moon in spring, and they observed Jesus's death on the Friday before, no matter when the Jewish community celebrated Passover that year; they ended their fasting period three days after Jesus's death, on Sunday morning. The inability to observe the death of Jesus, to establish a common fasting practice, and to celebrate his resurrection on the same date all over the Christian world, threatened the unity of the Catholic movement.[27] So, according to the Roman practice, Jesus died in a year when Passover fell on a Thursday, whereas the Asian practice assumed that Jesus died in a year when Passover fell on a Friday.

The first three gospel books of the Canonical Edition support the Roman practice, while the Gospel according to John supports the practice in Asia Minor. The editorial narrative, according to Irenaeus, indicates that Mark and Luke wrote their books in Rome, while John wrote his book in Ephesus. The Synoptics support the Roman storyline, and Gospel according to John endorses the tradition in Asia Minor. So, when Passover falls on a Thursday, as it does in Gospel according to John, this could not possibly be the same year indicated in the Synoptic Gospels when Passover fell on a Friday. The narrative discrepancy makes it impossible to determine the exact year of Jesus's death.

The two competing narratives, however, obscure not only the year of Jesus's death but also create confusion concerning the stories about the origin of the central ritual of the Catholic Christian movement, the Eucharist. The Asian tradition to commemorate Jesus's death at the time that the Passover lambs were ritually slaughtered supports the interpretation that Jesus died for the sins of humankind. The liturgy of the Eucharist, however, recalls Jesus's words at his "Last Supper," which was a Passover meal. Only one of these storylines can stand.

Advocating a compromise, in his letter to Victor, Bishop of Rome, Irenaeus reminded Victor of Polycarp's trip, when, several decades earlier, the same issue had been discussed between Polycarp and Anicetus.[28] Eusebius's statement that "Anicetus conceded the administration of the eucharist in the church to Polycarp," and that they celebrated communion together in Rome, illustrates the arrangement.

Irenaeus states that Anicetus followed the "customs of the presbyters" who had preceded him in Rome, and Polycarp based his tradition on "John the disciple of our Lord." Gospel according to John has the resurrected Christ celebrate his last meal when he appears at the shores of Lake Galilee and invites his followers using words reminiscent of the liturgical setting of the Eucharist: "Come and eat!" And Jesus "took the bread and gave it to them."[29]

That Anicetus and Polycarp "communed together" was a powerful symbolic gesture. Disagreements about liturgical practice should not divide the church. This also reflects the theological position of the publisher of the Canonical Edition, who presented the different Easter traditions next to each other, without alleviating discrepancies. It also gives the interpreter a valid answer on why the publisher of the Canonical Edition decided to feature four gospel books instead of one.

Polycarp of Smyrna's visit with Anicetus of Rome is a historical event that marks a conflict between the Catholic Christian leadership of Rome with leaders in Asia Minor and Greece. Historians agree that the meeting took place between 155 and 165, but the precise year is a matter of scholarly debate.[30] The Easter Controversy flared up again at the end of the second century and continued until 314, when, under the auspices of Emperor Constantine, the Council of Arles decided that Easter should be commemorated on the same day throughout the world.[31] Therefore, the unusual, and from a later perspective, unorthodox, solution of Polycarp and Anicetus, to let each region follow their own tradition, reflects an early stage of the Catholic discussion.

The message concerning the Easter Controversy was expressed by combining four gospel books into one literary unit, the Four-Gospel volume.[32] The position is not the message of a single book but reflects the conviction of the historical publisher of the collection.

• • •

The Canonical Edition of the New Testament is a clearly and consistently defined edition of twenty-seven writings organized in four volumes. The manuscript tradition reaches back to the second and third centuries.

Irenaeus described the Canonical Edition around 180. Justin's witness suggests its use in Catholic congregations before 161. Irenaeus's and Justin's testimony, together with Clement of Alexandria and Tertullian of Carthage, document international availability of the edition: Justin was born in Palestine and moved to Rome; Irenaeus grew up in Asia Minor, spent time in Rome, and became bishop in Lyons, modern-day France; Clement taught in Alexandria, Egypt; and Tertullian wrote from Carthage, North Africa.

These early documented readers experienced the Canonical Edition in distinction from and in competition with the Marcionite Edition. Because both editions used the same material, putting the texts to radically different ends, the two editions could not exist peacefully next to each other.

A promising approach to dating the Canonical Edition is to look for a historical conflict that the editorial framework of the edition faces and a conflict that is also documented in sources unrelated to the Canonical Edition.

The Easter Controversy between Catholic congregations in Rome and Asia Minor is just such a historical conflict. It is documented outside of the Canonical Edition. At some point between 155 and 165, Bishop Polycarp of Smyrna, representing congregations of Asia Minor, visited with Bishop Anicetus of Rome to discuss the matter. They decided to let every region follow their own traditions. The Canonical Edition promoted this solution as well. Gospels according to Mathew, Mark, and Luke supported Anicetus's tradition, and Gospel according to John supported Polycarp's tradition.

Judging from these four clusters of sources—(1) the manuscript evidence, (2) early documented readers, (3) the conflict with the Marcionite Edition, and (4) the Easter Controversy—the Canonical Edition was probably published before 161, but certainly before Irenaeus writes about it around the year 180. The event that may have triggered the first publication of the Canonical Edition of the New Testament may have been Polycarp's visit with Anicetus in Rome between 155 and 166.

During the second half of the second century, the Canonical Edition of the New Testament enters the stage of world literature as a publication in Greek for an international audience in Central Europe, North Africa, Asia Minor, and Greece.

III

WHAT DID COMPETING PUBLICATIONS LOOK LIKE?

BECAUSE THE CANONICAL EDITION of the New Testament has clearly defined editorial features, someone, somewhere, at a specific moment in time, must have gathered and published it. Available evidence points to the second half of the second century as the probable date of the Canonical Edition's appearance. And the same evidence points to the fact that the Canonical Edition faced competition. We know of at least one hundred books about Jesus and the apostles that are not part of the Christian Bible, all published before the end of the second century.[1]

The publisher of the Canonical Edition was aware that the Canonical Edition was only one of many works that tried to satisfy the public demand for books about the origin of the Christian movement. The last sentence of the Four-Gospel volume is: "But there are also many other things that Jesus did; if every one of them were written down, I suppose that the world itself could not contain the books that would be written" (John 21:25).

When the Canonical Edition is viewed as a second-century publication, a comparison with other books on Jesus produced in the second and third centuries can demonstrate typical features of the genre. Any of the characters or events recorded in these publications may be the product of someone's imagination. But even genres like fairy tales, utopias, and science fiction are written, edited, published, and read by real people who exist. Even if a story is pure fiction, the person who tells it is historical. We do not know whether Moby Dick, Robinson Crusoe, or Sherlock Holmes ever existed, but we do know who wrote and published the stories and how the reading public received them.

Literature becomes flesh when it is written down, edited, published, and read. And it leaves historical clues about authors, editors, publishers, and readers.

The following examples of publications on Jesus that were on the market at the time the Canonical Edition was published and found its readers are chosen for the purpose of illustrating certain aspects they share: critical engagement with Jewish scriptural traditions, infatuation with book publishing, using the authoritative voices of first-century witnesses to address second-century problems, fixation on the creation narratives of Genesis, filling in narrative gaps in the tradition, creating historical credibility by referencing seemingly independent sources, and producing edited collections of apostolic writings to promote a narrative—to name but a few of their generic properties. These publications typically address an audience that seeks authoritative information that has been hidden from the public.[2]

They share a metanarrative that explains where Christ came from, what he did and taught while he was on earth, and what happened after Christ returned to the spiritual realm from which he had made his descent.

§4
Diverse Examples

Secret Book of John

Secret Book of John presents itself as a manuscript written by the disciple John in which he recorded a conversation with the "Savior." The voice of the publisher introduces and concludes John's narrative, which is written in the first-person singular.[3]

> *The teaching of the Savior, and [the revelation] of the
> mysteries [and the things] hidden in silence, things he taught
> his disciple John.*
>
> *One day when John the brother of James, who are the
> sons of Zebedee, went up to the temple, it happened that a*

*Pharisee named Arimanios came up to him and said to him,
"Where is your teacher, whom you followed?" I said to him,
"He has returned to the place he came from." The Pharisee
said to me, "This Nazarene really has deceived you, filled your
ears with lies, closed [your minds], and turned you from the
traditions of your ancestors."*

*When I, John, heard this, I turned away from the
temple and went to a mountainous and barren place. I
was distressed within, and I asked how the* Savior *was
chosen: Why was he sent into the world by his Father? Who
is his Father who sent him? (NHC II, 1: 1; Meyer,* Nag
Hammadi, *107)*

This first scene pits John against the cynical comments of a Pharisee who ridicules John because Jesus had died. John, deeply troubled,
retreats to a barren place, and the Savior reveals himself to John.

A few chapters later, the Savior tells John how "Yaldabaoth"
was born. Yaldabaoth is a child of Sophia, which "she conceived of a
thought from herself" and "without the consent of the Spirit."[4]

*Something came out of her that was imperfect and different
in appearance from her, for she had produced it without her
partner. It did not resemble its mother and was misshapen.
When Sophia saw what her desire had produced, it changed
into the figure of a snake with the face of a lion. Its eyes were
like flashing bolts of lightning. . . . She named her offspring*
Yaldabaoth. *(NHC II, 1: 10; Meyer,* Nag Hammadi, *115)*

When the Savior, who tells the story, recounts the creation of Adam
and Eve, he does not hesitate to correct the story in Genesis: "It did not
happen, however, the way Moses said."

*The first ruler removed part of Adam's power and created
another figure in the form of a female, like the image of
Insight that had appeared to him. He put the part he*

had taken from the power of the human being into the
female creature. It did not happen, however, the way
Moses said: "Adam's rib." (NHC II, 1: 22–23 Meyer,
Nag Hammadi, *126)*

What really happened was, according to the Savior, that Yaldabaoth, the first ruler, raped Eve. She gave birth to Yahweh and Elohim, which Moses in his account calls Cain and Abel.

The first ruler defiled Eve and produced in her two sons, a
first and a second: Elohim and Yahweh. Elohim has the face
of a bear; Yahweh has the face of a cat. One is just, the other
is unjust. He placed Yahweh over fire and wind, he placed
Elohim over water and earth. He called them by the names
Cain and Abel, with a view to deceive. To this day sexual
intercourse has persisted because of the first ruler. He planted
sexual desire within the woman who belongs to Adam.
Through intercourse the first ruler produced duplicate bodies,
and he blew some of his false spirit into them. (NHC II, 1:
24; Meyer, Nag Hammadi, *127–128)*

At the end of the book, the Savior commands John to write everything down and to share the message only with his spiritual friends. Readers understand that they are receiving privileged information that has been hidden from the public eye.

Not the voice of the author, however, but the publisher's voice concludes the book. The publisher talks about the manuscript of John and provides a short provenance narrative.

This is the mystery of the unshakable generation. The Savior
communicated this to John for him to record and safeguard.
He said to him, "Cursed be anyone who will trade these
things for a gift, for food, drink, clothes, or anything [32]
like this." These things were communicated to him in a

mystery, and at once the Savior disappeared. Then John went to the other disciples *and reported what the Savior had told him. Jesus Christ Amen. The Secret Book According to John. (NHC II, 1: 31:25–32:10; Meyer,* Nag Hammadi*, 132)*

Before its publication, the manuscript had circulated only among "the other disciples," which explains why readers had not heard of this work before. They were not allowed to make copies and sell these revelations for "a gift, food, drink, clothes, or anything like this," but after the death of the last disciple, this command became obsolete. Readers now have the privilege to read the secret book as a publication, and they will have to pay for a copy of the first edition.

Engagement with Jewish Scriptures

Tertullian, who promoted the Old Testament of the Canonical Edition, opposed the concept of a lesser god than the God of Israel who was to blame for all imperfections of creation. *Secret Book of John* demonstrates why. Stories explaining the origin of this lesser god must correct the creation story in Genesis, and these corrections undermine the authority of Jewish Scriptures. To identify Cain and Abel with Elohim and Yahweh, fathered by the Demiurge who raped Eve, denies that the god who created the first human beings could possibly be the Father of Jesus.

On the other hand, using the disciple John as the authoritative voice and publishing his eyewitness report shows that *Secret Book of John* seeks a place among Christians and in the library of Christian writings.

Holy Book of the Great Invisible Spirit

The imperfect god who created the world is often referred to as the Demiurge. I use the term in this sense. The Greek word literally means someone who works for the public, a craftsman, or artisan. The concept of a perfect Divinity, who gave life to lesser gods who then created the material world, is already found in the writings of Plato.[5]

The anonymous narrator of *The Holy Book of the Great Invisible Spirit* takes the concept of the Demiurge, who is named Sakla in this story, and runs with it.[6] Sakla was delusional and thought that he had created everything, including the first human.

> *After [the world] was founded, Sakla said to his [angels], "I am a [jealous] god, and nothing has [come into being] apart from me." [He] felt certain of his nature.*
>
> *A voice called from on high and said, "Humankind exists, and the Son of Man."*
>
> *The first modeled creature was formed from the descent of the image above. The image resembles its voice on high, the voice of the image. The image gazed out, and from the gaze of the image above, the first creature was formed. And for the sake of this creature* repentance *came to be. "Repentance" was completed and empowered through the will and good pleasure of the father. (NHC III, 2, 58–59; Meyer,* Gnostic Gospels, *133)*

The first human creature, however, was formed from "the gaze of the image above," the narrator insists, when the image briefly peeked down from heaven before the Demiurge did his work. This Great Invisible Spirit was merciful and provided human beings with a chance for "repentance," setting up the storyline of salvation for humans through the ministry of Jesus the Christ. The book ends with a baptismal hymn.

Concept of the Demiurge

Although the Canonical Edition supports the concept of angels, demons, Satan, and other divine powers in heaven, it opposes the idea of a lesser god when it comes to interpreting the creation narratives of Genesis. The perfect God, the divine Father of Jesus the Christ, the God of Abraham, Jacob, and Isaac created the world and the first human beings. The Canonical Edition reacts to a well-documented conflict within the Christian movement, just as Justin, Irenaeus, Tertullian, and Clement of Alexandria had experienced it.

Gospel of Truth

The unnamed narrator of the *Gospel of Truth* expresses confidence in being fully informed of what Jesus did and taught. The narrator references events in the life of Jesus but does not report them, assuming that readers were familiar with a basic narrative of Jesus.[7]

> *He became a way for* those who strayed, knowledge *for those who were ignorant, discovery* for those who sought, *support for those who tremble, purity for those who were defiled. (NHC I, 3, 31; Meyer,* Nag Hammadi, *42)*

Only the outcome of Jesus's ministry is reviewed: Jesus redeemed "those who strayed," conveyed "knowledge" for the ignorant, gave insight "for those who sought."

> *In their hearts the living* book *of the living was revealed, the* book *that was written in the father's thought and mind and was,* since the foundation of all, *in his incomprehensible nature. No one had been able to take up this* book, *since it was ordained that the one who would take it up would be slain. And nothing could appear among those who believed in salvation unless that* book *had come out. For this reason, the merciful, faithful Jesus was patient and accepted his sufferings to the point of taking up that* book, *since he knew that his death would be life for many. (NHC I, 3, 19–20; Meyer,* Nag Hammadi, *38)*

The writer assumes that readers are familiar with "book" production and promotion. The crucifixion of Jesus is compared to the publication of a book that had existed "since the foundation of all" in the incomprehensible nature of the father's thought.[8]

> *Jesus appeared, put on that book, was nailed to a tree, and* published the father's edict *on the cross. Oh, what a great*

> *teaching! He humbled himself even unto death, though*
> *clothed in eternal life. He stripped off the perishable rags and*
> *clothed himself in incorruptibility, which no one can take*
> *from him. (NHC I, 3, 20; Meyer, Nag Hammadi, 38)*

Through his sufferings on the cross, Jesus "published the father's edict."

Book Publishing Culture

The author of the *Gospel of Truth* used the concept of a published book to explain Jesus's crucifixion. Author and readers share a culture in which books are understood to communicate knowledge internationally and timelessly, from one generation to the next.

The Canonical Edition of the New Testament, providing the testimony of first-century authors to second-century readers, uses the same cultural concept that only a society familiar with authoring, editing, publishing, selling, buying, and reading books could understand.

Secret Book of James

The Coptic version of *Secret Book of James* forms the second tractate of Codex I of the Nag Hammadi library.[9] The implied author, James, writes a confidential letter to convey his message.[10]

> *[James] writes to. . . . Peace be [with you from] peace,*
> *[love] from love, [grace] from grace, [faith] from faith, life*
> *from holy life. You have asked me to send you a secret book*
> *revealed to me and* Peter *by the* master, *and I could not turn*
> *you down, nor could I speak to you, so [I have written] it in*
> *Hebrew and have sent it to you, and* to you alone. *(NHC I,*
> *2:1; Meyer, Nag Hammadi, 23)*

The implied publisher made sure that readers understood that the text was based on a Hebrew autograph and that only one exemplar existed. Familiarity with a narrative of Jesus and his twelve disciples was presumed. He expected readers to know who "James" was, who "Peter" was, and who "the master" was. The expression "sent to you alone" signals to implied readers of the publication that only one copy existed and that the publisher had accessed this document.

> *But since you are a minister of the salvation of the saints, do your best to be careful not to communicate to many people this book that the Savior did not want to communicate even to all of us, his* twelve disciples. *Nonetheless, blessed will they be who will be saved through the faith of this treatise. (NHC I, 2:1; Meyer,* Nag Hammadi*, 23)*

Readers learn that the author, James, was one of the "twelve disciples," and that James had asked the recipient of this letter not to share the content with anyone, not even with the other disciples of Jesus.

> *The twelve disciples were all sitting together, recalling what the savior had said to each of them, whether* in a hidden or an open manner*, and organizing it in books. I was writing what is in [my book]. (NHC I, 2:1; Meyer,* Nag Hammadi*, 24)*

The opening scene depicts the twelve disciples of Jesus sitting together, each one writing their own book about what they remember.[11] The expression "in a hidden or an open manner" conveys the notion that Jesus sometimes communicated with the individual disciple in private and expected the disciple to keep whatever Jesus had told him to himself.[12]

Then the resurrected Lord appears.

> *Look, the Savior appeared, after he had left [us, while we] were watching for him.* Five hundred fifty days after he rose from the dead, *we said to him, "Did you depart and leave us?" Jesus said, "No, but I shall return to the place from which I came." (NHC I, 2:2; Meyer,* Nag Hammadi*, 24)*

An appearance of Jesus 550 days after his resurrection is quite different from the storyline of other books about Jesus.

Speeches of the resurrected Christ, however, create a set of narrative problems. If Jesus was brought back from the realms of death to receive eternal life, where is he now? To discourage the obvious conclusion that the carpenter from Nazareth must have died a second time, an ascension story resolves the narrative conflict.

> *This is all I shall tell you at this time. Now I shall ascend to*
> the place from which *I have come. . . . When he said this, he*
> left. *Peter and I knelt down, gave thanks, and sent our hearts*
> *up to heaven. We heard with our ears and saw with our*
> *eyes* the noise of wars, a trumpet blast, and great turmoil.
> *(NHC I, 2:15; Meyer,* Nag Hammadi, *29–30)*

The Secret Book of James provides a scene in which disciples witness Jesus's return to heaven. James heard and saw "noise of wars, a trumpet blast, and great turmoil" after Jesus returned to "the place from which" he came. Divine powers in heaven are fighting each other.

Edition Based on Autograph
James, one of the twelve disciples of Jesus, tells the story with the authority of an eyewitness. He received privileged information that he shared with only one person, the recipient of the letter. The implied publisher suggested that this book was published from James's original document.

Gospel according to Mary

This gospel book features the voice of a certain Mary by capturing conversations that took place after Jesus's death and resurrection.[13]

> *When the blessed one said this, he greeted all of them and*
> *said, "Peace be with you. Receive my peace. Be careful that*

no one leads you astray by saying, 'Look here' or 'Look there.'
The child of humankind is within you. Follow that. Those
who seek it will find it. Go and preach the good news of
the kingdom. *Do not lay down any rules other than what I*
have given you, and do not establish law, as the lawgiver did,
or you will be bound by it." When he said this, he left them.
(BG 8502, 8; Meyer, Gospels, *38)*

The wish of peace, warnings of false Messiahs, the self-designation of
Jesus as Son of man, the notion that the experience of Jesus is now a
spiritual experience, the promise that "those who seek it will find it,"
the commissioning to "preach the good news of the kingdom," and the
reference to Jesus's departure are familiar elements of the Jesus story
that are also found in other gospel books. The solemn admonishment,
however, "Do not lay down any rules other than what I have given
you," is different. It prepares readers for the dialogue between Peter
and Mary. Using the first-person plural, "we," Peter speaks for all male
disciples.

> *Peter said to Mary, "Sister, we know the savior loved you*
> *more than any other woman. Tell us the words of the*
> *savior that you remember, which you know but we do not,*
> *because we have not heard them." (BG 8502, 10; Meyer,*
> Gospels, *38)*

And Mary responds.

> *She began to speak these words to them. She said, "*I saw the
> master in a vision, *and I said to him, 'Master, today I saw*
> *you in a vision.' "He answered and said to me, 'Blessings on*
> *you, since you did not waver at the sight of me. For where*
> *the mind is, the treasure is.' "I said to him, 'Master, how does*
> *a person see a vision, with the soul or with the spirit?' "The*
> *savior answered and said, 'A person sees neither with the soul*

> *nor with the spirit. The mind, which is between the two, sees*
> *the vision.'" (BG 8502, 10; Meyer,* Gospels, *38–39)*

Mary's revelation is based on a visionary experience that no one else had witnessed. After listening to Mary, the disciples Andrew and Peter wondered whether this vision was relevant to anyone but Mary.

> *When Mary said this, she became silent, since the savior had*
> *spoken this much to her. Andrew answered and said to the*
> *brothers, "Say what you think about what she said, but I*
> *do not believe the savior said this. These teachings certainly*
> *are strange ideas." Peter voiced similar concerns. He asked*
> *the others about the savior: "Did he really speak with a*
> *woman in private, without our knowledge? Should we all*
> *turn and listen to her? Did he prefer her to us?" Then Mary*
> *wept and said to Peter, "My brother Peter, what do you*
> *think? Do you think that* I *made this up by myself or that*
> I am *lying about the savior?" (BG 8502, 17–18; Meyer,*
> Gospels, *40–42)*

Mary poses a central question: Are visions something a spiritual person "makes up"? Would such a person be "lying about the savior"? These questions are probably rhetorical questions, expecting an answer along the lines that a spiritual experience is not a lie. But if visions and revelations of Jesus are relevant to understanding the message of God, gender should not make a difference. Or should it?

Levi comes to Mary's rescue, as he is convinced that Jesus did not deny women the authority to lead a community. Levi argues that the rule that allowed only men to pastor a congregation had been introduced recently, by people like Peter and Andrew.

> *Levi answered and said to Peter, "Peter, you always are angry.*
> *Now I see you arguing against this woman like an adversary.*

*If the savior made her worthy, who are you to reject her?
Surely the savior knows her well. That is why he has loved her
more than us. So, we should be ashamed and put on perfect
humanity and acquire it, as he commanded us, and preach
the good news, not making any rule or law other than what
the savior indicated." When [Levi said] this, they began to
leave [in order to] teach and preach. (BG 8502, 18; Meyer,*
Gospels, *42)*[14]

In another version of the *Gospel of Mary*, only Levi went out to preach; the other apostles did not follow, and the conflict between Levi and his two colleagues Peter and Andrew was not resolved.[15]

Addressing Social Conflict
The gospel book of Mary addresses a social conflict of the second century, the question of whether the spiritual experience of women is just as genuine as the spiritual experience of men, and whether women can provide spiritual leadership in Christian faith communities. This timeless discussion is presented in the voices of first-century characters: Mary, Peter, Andrew, and Levi.[16]

Dialogue of the Savior

The *Dialogue of the Savior* features the voices of Mary, Judas, and Matthew.

The savior *said to* his disciples, *"Now the time has come,
brothers and sisters, for us to leave our labor behind and
stand at rest, for whoever stands at rest will rest forever."*
(NHC III, 5:120; Meyer, Gospels, *225)*

The opening sentence assumes that readers know who "the Savior" is and who "his disciples" are. These characters have positive connotations and readers are expected to identify with them. A text like this could only be understood if a shared narrative existed that needed no further explanations.

> *Judas said, "Tell [us], master, what [existed] before [heaven and] earth came into being?" The master said, "There was* darkness *and* water, *and* spirit *upon [water]. And I tell you [the truth], look, what you seek and inquire about [is] within you, and it [has] the power and mystery [of the] spirit, for [it is] from [the spirit].* Wickedness *entered [in order to destroy] the mind, [forever]." (NHC III, 5:127–128; Meyer,* Gospels, *228–229)*

The narrator's references to "earth," "darkness," "water," and "spirit" hovering over it point readers to the opening sentences of the creation accounts in Genesis. And that "wickedness" is part of the human mind is presented as an undisputable fact.

> *Mary asked, "[Of what] kind is the* mustard seed? *Is it from heaven or from earth?" The master said, "When the father established the world for himself, he left many things with the* mother of all. *That is why he sows and works." (NHC III, 5:144; Meyer,* Gospels, *238)*

For readers of the Canonical Edition references to the parable of the mustard seed, the parable of the sower, and the first creation story, in which God rested for a day after working for six days, may feel familiar. The narrator assumes that God the Father did not create every detail of creation, suggesting another divine power responsible for everything that went wrong. In this text, the Demiurge is called "mother of all."

> *Judas said, "How is the spirit disclosed?" The master said, "How [is] the sword [disclosed]?" Judas said, "How is the light disclosed?" The master said, "[It is disclosed] through itself eternally." (NHC III, 5:146; Meyer,* Gospels, *240)*

The Spirit is understood as being self-evident. The Spirit is experienced the same way a sword is felt, or light is perceived; a personal event and yet shared with everyone who touched a sword, saw the light, or received the Spirit.

> *Mary asked her brothers, "Where are you going to store [these]*
> *questions you ask of the child of [humankind]?" The master*
> *[said] to her, "Sister, [no one] can ask about these things*
> *[except] someone* who has a place to store them in the heart.
> *And such a person can leave [the world] and enter the place*
> *[of life] and will* not be held back in this world of poverty."
> *(NHC III, 5:131–132; Meyer,* Gospels, *230–231)*

When Mary asks the apostles where they are going to keep a record of their questions, Jesus answers that only someone who has "a place to store them in the heart" will "not be held back in this world of poverty."[17]

Shared Narrative and Recurring Themes
Dialogue of the Savior combines several themes that are encountered in other writings about Jesus and his apostles.

Using the voice of an omniscient narrator and featuring prominent first-century followers of Jesus, the tractate assumes a shared narrative world that allowed disciples to interact with their Lord and endorsed spiritual experiences as an accepted way to understand and interpret the teachings of Jesus. The question of whether the God of Jesus was also the creator of the world displays a fascination with the creation story found in Genesis. The answer that the Lord did not create every detail and that "he left many things with the mother of all" gives a feminine touch to the concept of the Demiurge.

Promoting the idea that secret teachings are stored in the hearts of believers, who in this case are the readers of this tractate, the book endorses the role of book publishing, a medium that transverses time and place and communicates eternal truth from one spiritual person to the heart of another one.

Infancy Gospel of James

The implied author of the *Infancy Gospel of James* introduces himself as the older brother of Jesus at the end of the book.[18]

> *But I James, the one who has written this account in Jerusalem, hid myself away in the wilderness when there was a disturbance* at the death of Herod, *until the disturbance in Jerusalem came to an end. There I glorified God, the Master, who gave me the gift and the wisdom to write this account. (InfJames 25; Ehrman,* Scriptures, *71–72)*

The final passage informs readers that James wrote the book when Jesus was still a baby, at the time that Herod died.[19]

One of the narrative discrepancies between Gospel according to Matthew and Gospel according to Luke is Matthew's story that Herod "killed all the children in and around Bethlehem who were two years old or under" (Matt 2:16). Gospel according to Luke tells the story of Mary visiting Elizabeth, who is pregnant with John the Baptist.[20] So why did King Herod not kill John the Baptist? The *Infancy Gospel of James* addressed the narrative conflict and added a story of how John was miraculously saved.

> *When Herod realized that he had been mocked by the wise men, he grew angry and sent murderers, saying to them, "Kill every infant, two years and under." When Mary heard that the infants were being killed, out of fear she* took her child and wrapped him in swaddling clothes and placed him in a cattle manger. *But when Elizabeth heard that they were looking for John, she took him and went up into the mountains, looking for a place to hide him. But there was no hiding place. Elizabeth moaned and said with a loud voice, "Mountain of God, receive a mother with her child." For Elizabeth was not able to climb the mountain. And straight away the mountain split open and received her. And a light*

was shining around them, for an angel of the Lord was with
them, protecting them. (InfJames 22; Ehrman, Scriptures, *71)*

Only readers who are familiar with both infancy narratives, the one
reflected in Gospel according to Matthew and the one reflected in
Gospel according to Luke, will wonder about the survival of John the
Baptist. The narrative solution given by James's gospel book, however,
comes at a price. It differs from Matthew's storyline that has Mary
and Joseph following the advice of an angel and escaping to Egypt
unharmed by Herod's wrath.[21] Instead, Mary "took her child and
wrapped him in swaddling clothes and placed him in a cattle manger."

Filling in Narrative Gaps
The *Infancy Gospel of James* answers numerous other questions in his
gospel book by providing episodes not contained in the Canonical
Edition. For example, how could Mary have been born without sin?
Answer: Mary's mother, Anna, conceived without having sex (chapter
4). How could Jesus be Mary's only child if he had brothers and sisters?
Answer: The other children were from Joseph's first marriage (chapter
8). How could one know that Mary was a virgin even after giving
birth? Answer: A miracle. After the birth of Jesus, skeptical Salome
performed a medical exam, and she found Mary to still be a virgin
(chapter 20). The assessment of Mary's virginity is not consistent with
Gospel according to Matthew, which clearly communicates that Mary
and Joseph had intercourse after Jesus was born.[22]

Any story may have happened or may be the figment of someone's
imagination, but the publishers and readers, their questions and their literary output, are a matter of historical record. Whether Mary was a virgin before and after birth cannot be established with historical methods;
but that the question was asked and that the answers mattered during
the second, third, and fourth centuries can be documented beyond reasonable doubt through James's gospel book and its transmission.

If James, the older brother of Jesus, gives a record of the most
intimate details only a family member could know, his testimony

provides more credibility to the narrative than the witness of a tax collector and disciple of Jesus, like Matthew, or a medical doctor and follower of Paul, like Luke. Narrative inconsistencies were common in publications about Jesus, and ironically, correcting the shared narrative, elaborating details, and filling in gaps increases the credibility.

Stories of Christ's Childhood
Infancy Gospel of Thomas

This book with stories from Christ's childhood did not disclose its author in the title. The first printed edition used a late Greek version, which called the book the Infancy Gospel of Thomas. But the term *gospel* and the attribution to Thomas is not part of the earliest tradition.[23] Irenaeus referred to a story about Jesus chastising his teacher and, because a similar episode is contained in this gospel book, some interpreters suggest that the book was published during or before the middle of the second century.[24]

The first sentence gives the age of Jesus as five years old.

> *When this child Jesus was* five years old, *he was playing by the ford of a stream; and he gathered the flowing waters into pools and made them immediately pure. These things he ordered* simply by speaking a word. *(InfThomas 2:1; Ehrman, Scriptures, 58)*

By letting the boy Jesus change nature through oral commands, the narrator references the first creation story in Genesis, where God created the world "simply by speaking a word."

When Joseph found himself in a conundrum because he had cut off a board too short, Jesus helps his father to fix the problem by miraculously stretching the board.

> Now his father *was a carpenter*, and at that time he used to make plows and yokes. He received an order from a certain rich man to make a bed. But when the measurement for

one of the beautiful crossbeams came out too short, he
did not know what to do. The child Jesus said to his father
Joseph, "Place the two pieces of wood on the floor and line
them up from the middle to one end." Joseph did just as
the child said. Then Jesus stood at the other end, grabbed
the shorter board, and stretched it out to make it the same
length as the other. His father Joseph saw what he had
done and was amazed. He embraced the child and gave
him a kiss, saying "I am blessed that God has given me this
child." (InfThomas 13:1–2; Ehrman, *Scriptures*, 60–61)

Again, the narrator assumes that readers are familiar with a metanarrative in which Joseph and Mary are the parents of Jesus and Joseph "was a carpenter."

The episodes sometimes carry a humoristic note, like the story referenced by Irenaeus about Jesus and his teacher, which leaves Jesus's father, Joseph, at his wits' end.[25]

> *Then Jesus said to him, "If you are really a teacher and know*
> *the letters well, tell me the power of the Alpha, and I will tell*
> *you the power of the Beta." The teacher was aggravated and*
> *struck him on the head. The child was hurt and cursed him;*
> *and immediately he fainted and fell to the ground on his face.*
> *The child returned to Joseph's house. Joseph was smitten with*
> *grief and ordered his mother, "Do not let him out the door;*
> *for those who anger him die." (InfThomas 14:2–3; Ehrman,*
> Scriptures, *61)*

The theme to portray Joseph as a well-intentioned father who is overwhelmed by the boy's actions and to portray Mary as the one responsible for the upbringing of the child brings the book to a conclusion. The narrative ends with the twelve-year-old Jesus in the temple, which is also found in Luke's Gospel. On their way home from Jerusalem, the parents realize that their son was not with them.[26]

InfThomas 19:2–4	Luke 2:44–50
After their first day of travel, they began looking for him among their relatives and were upset not to find him. They returned again to the city to look for him. And after the third day they found him sitting in the Temple in the midst of the teachers, both listening and asking them questions. Everyone was attending closely, amazed that though a child, he questioned the elders and teachers of the people sharply, <u>explaining the chief points of the Law and the parables of the prophets.</u>	Assuming that he was in the group of travelers, they went a day's journey. Then they started to look for him among their relatives and friends. When they did not find him, they returned to Jerusalem to search for him. After three days they found him in the temple, sitting among the teachers, listening to them and asking them questions. And all who heard him were amazed at his understanding and his answers.
When his mother Mary came up to him she said, "Why have you done this to us, child? See, we have been distressed, looking for you." Jesus replied to them, "Why are you looking for me? Don't you know that I must be with those who are my Father's?" <u>The scribes and Pharisees said, "Are you the mother of this child?" She replied, "I am." They said to her, "You are most fortunate among women, because God has blessed the fruit of your womb. For we have never seen or heard of such glory, such virtue and wisdom."</u>	When ~~his parents saw him they were astonished; and~~ his mother said to him, "Child, why have you treated us like this? Look, your father and I have been searching for you in great anxiety." He said to them, "Why were you searching for me? Did you not know that I must be in my Father's house?" ~~But they did not understand what he said to them.~~

The story is similar but not identical to the one in Gospel according to Luke. The anonymous Infancy Gospel highlights Mary's role and diminishes Joseph's role even more than Gospel according to Luke.

Suggesting Independent Traditions

Reading two similar accounts with slight differences leaves readers with the impression that the stories are based on independent traditions, suggesting that the similarities prove the historical value of the narrative. And once the credibility of a witness is established, whatever this voice adds to the familiar account will be received as truth as well.

As in James's gospel book, the birth and early childhood of Jesus is a topic of interest to publishers and readers in the second century.[27]

Second Discourse of Great Seth

Second Discourse of Great Seth presents the narrative in the first-person singular from Christ's point of view. Heaven is a place where the forces of good and evil fight each other. The protagonist, Christ, is surrounded by opposing powers but outwits them and, through shape-shifting and his unbreakable will, he escapes and passes through the heavenly gates.

> *I brought all their powers into subjection. When I came down, no one saw me, for I kept changing my forms on high, transforming from shape to shape, so when I was at their gates, I assumed their likeness. I passed by them quietly. I saw their realms, but I was not afraid or ashamed, because I was pure. I was speaking with them and mingling with them, through those who are mine. Jealously I trampled on those who are harsh toward them, and I put out the fire. I was doing all this by my will, to complete what I willed in the will of the Father above.* (NHC VII, 2:56–57; Meyer, Nag Hammadi, 480)

Christ then slips into a human body, "evicting the previous occupant," to accomplish his Father's mission.

> *I approached a bodily dwelling and* evicted the previous
> occupant, *and I went in. The whole multitude of archons was*
> *upset, and all the material stuff of the rulers and the powers*
> *born of earth began to tremble at the sight of the figure with a*
> *composite image. I was in it, and I did not look like the previous*
> *occupant. He was a worldly person, but I, I am from above the*
> *heavens. I did not defy them, and I became an anointed one,*
> *but neither did I reveal myself to them in the love coming from*
> *me. Rather, I revealed that I am a stranger to the regions below.*
> *(NHC VII, 2:51–52; Meyer,* Nag Hammadi, *478)*

When Christ is nailed to the cross, he looks down at those who thought they had defeated him and is "laughing at their ignorance."

> *They nailed their man to their death. Their thoughts did not*
> *perceive me, since they were deaf and blind. By doing these*
> *things they pronounce judgment against themselves. As for me,*
> *they saw me and punished me, but someone else, their father,*
> *drank the gall and the vinegar; it was not I. They were striking*
> *me with a scourge, but someone else, Simon, bore the cross on*
> *his shoulder. Someone else wore the crown of thorns. And I was*
> *on high, poking fun at all the excesses of the rulers and the fruit*
> *of their error and conceit. I was laughing at their ignorance.*
> *(NHC VII, 2:55–56; Meyer,* Nag Hammadi, *480)*

Christ then travels to Hades and returns to heaven by his own will.

Narrator's Perspective

Choosing a specific narrative perspective, often the perspective of a close follower of Jesus, to convey the secret message of Christ is a common strategy of the genre. The author of *Second Discourse of Great Seth* eliminates the person who witnesses the events and makes Christ the narrator, who tells the story of what happened in heaven before he entered the body of a man, how he experienced human life and death, and how he returned to his divine Father.

Marcionite Edition

The Marcionite Edition consists of ten letters of Paul and one gospel book. It has not survived in manuscripts. Nevertheless, readers critically discussed the gospel book in so much detail that it can be reconstructed with a high degree of scholarly consensus. The text of the letters, however, is not attested very well.[28]

The scholarly consensus assumes that the title of the gospel book was simply "Gospel." The first letter presented in the collection of Paul's letters is a letter to Galatians. In the first passage of this letter, Paul denounces the authority of any other gospel book. In no uncertain words, Paul expresses his disgust at anyone who might turn "to a different gospel" than "what you received." Even if "we or an angel from heaven should proclaim to you a gospel contrary to what we proclaimed to you, let that one be accursed!"[29]

The editorial narrative of the Marcionite Edition presents its gospel book as the only acceptable one, denouncing all others as fakes, and therefore stands in stark contrast to the editorial narrative of the Canonical Edition, which promotes four gospel books.

Gospel
The first and the last sentences of the Marcionite Gospel provide a simple frame. Jesus enters the story without further introduction as he goes down to Capharnaum (Capernaum) and he leaves from Jerusalem at the end of the book.[30]

> *3,1a In the 15th year of the reign of Emperor Tiberius, 4,31 {Jesus} went down to Capharnaum, a city in Galilee {at the sea in the territory of Zebulon and Naphtali}. (*Ev 3:1a; 4:31)*

The beginning of Jesus's public presence is clearly dated to "the 15th year of the reign of Emperor Tiberius." Tiberius was installed by the Senate in Rome on 18 September 14, indicating to educated readers that the story begins between September of 29 and September of 30. The story ends on the Sunday following Passover when the resurrected Christ leaves Jerusalem; no corresponding year is given.

Although there are no stories about what Jesus did before he arrived in Capharnaum, the anonymous narrator informs readers that Jesus grew up in Nazareth, and he is referred to once as "Jesus the Nazorean."[31] His father is called Joseph, and in one episode his mother and his brothers are mentioned, but no names are given.[32] Jesus lived in Capharnaum.[33]

The stories follow each other in an episodic fashion. Jesus travels in the region but always returns to Capharnaum. At some point, he begins to travel toward Jerusalem, where he dies and where he appears to his followers as the resurrected Christ.

The passion story is told without an elaborate timeline. Jesus comes to Jerusalem and teaches regularly in the temple. Readers are informed that "the day of unleavened bread, which is called the Passover, was near."[34] A few sentences later they are told, "the day of Passover came on which the Passover lamb had to be slaughtered." Jesus is crucified the day following the Passover dinner, a Friday.[35]

The story ends with the discovery of the empty tomb the following Sunday morning. Jesus appears twice, once in the afternoon and once in the evening, and "departed from them" late Sunday night from "Bethany."

> [50]*But he led them out to Bethany. And lifting up his hands he blessed them. {And he sent out the apostles to proclaim to all the Gentile nations.}* [51]*And it happened when he blessed them that he departed from them.* [52]*And they returned to Jerusalem full of joy.* [53]*And they praised God at all times.* (*Ev 24:50–53)

The narrative perspective of this gospel book is the perspective of an authoritative, omniscient narrator and is consistent with the messaging of the editorial narrative that Paul had not written the gospel book, only "handed on" what he "in turn had received."[36]

Letters of Paul
The sequence of the letters of Paul in the Marcionite Edition was as follows: a letter to Galatians, two letters to Corinthians, a letter to Romans, two letters to Thessalonians, and a letter each to Laodiceans, Colossians, Philippians, and to Philemon. The letters are arranged chronologically.[37]

The story covers roughly twelve months and takes readers from Damascus to Rome. The plot is driven by the conflict between Paul and his rivals, the disciples of Jesus and the brothers of Jesus. A letter to Galatians sets the stage by explaining that Paul traveled from Damascus to Jerusalem, where Jesus's brother James and Jesus's disciples John and Peter asked him to raise money for the poor in Jerusalem. Shortly after this meeting, Paul clashes with Peter in Antioch. The two letters to Corinthians document how Paul's fundraising campaign was sabotaged by the hostile followers of the "super-apostles" Peter and the brothers of Jesus (who are explicitly mentioned in the first and referenced in the second letter), as Paul made his way from Antioch via Ephesus and Macedonia to Corinth. From Corinth he sends a letter to Romans and two letters to Thessalonians. Paul writes the remaining four letters to Laodiceans, Colossians, Philippians, and Philemon from captivity in Rome. The trip took about one year, and the story is open ended, the conflict between Peter and Paul remaining unresolved.[38]

In the second century, when Paul's letters are read as part of the Marcionite Edition, Paul the apostle becomes a role model for readers who never met Jesus of Nazareth and who base their identity exclusively on a spiritual experience of Christ. Like Paul, they only know of Jesus from literature. In his letters, Paul explains that Christ was sent by his Father, died as Jesus on the cross, and returned to heaven, from where he shall return soon to judge the living and the dead. Experiencing Christ supersedes experiencing Jesus. Paul trumps Peter. Christianity is born.

Edited Collection

The Marcionite Edition tells its story by selecting ten letters of Paul, giving them titles, arranging them in a specific order, and publishing them alongside the gospel book.[39] The protagonist of the plot is Paul; the antagonists are the disciples of Jesus and the brothers of Jesus. Just as the gospel book only covers a limited period in Jesus's life, the letters also only cover a limited period in Paul's life.[40]

This editorial narrative is not a historical assessment. One should not assume that any publisher would publish any letters without editorial changes just because an edition implies the use of autographs. A letter in an edited collection may reflect a historical letter or it may be fictitious. No editorial narrative should be taken as historically reliable without independent confirmation.

Although the historical accuracy of the letters or the gospel book cannot be assessed, the message of the historical publisher is easy to grasp. The publisher of the Marcionite Edition told readers (1) that a certain Paul was the author of the letters, (2) that the selection, titles, and arrangement of the letters reflected Paul's intentions, and (3) that the gospel book was the one Paul had received and promoted.

If *New Covenant [New Testament]* was the title of the Marcionite Edition, as some scholars have suggested, it reflected Paul's remark that he, the main contributing author to the collection, and his associates are "ministers of a new covenant."[41]

> *Not that we are competent of ourselves to claim anything as coming from us; our competence is from God, who has made us competent to be* ministers of a new covenant *[= New Testament], not of letter but of spirit; for the letter kills, but the Spirit gives life. (Marcionite Edition, 2 Corinthians 3:5–6)*

And when Paul states that he passed on the gospel book that he had received, the letters function as an endorsement of God's call to publish it. In his own words, God enabled Paul and his followers, which certainly includes the publisher of the Marcionite Edition and hopefully also its readers, to the ministry of promoting the gospel book called New Testament. The full title of the Marcionite Edition therefore could be paraphrased as "New Covenant according to Paul."

§5
Shared Features

Shared Narrative

Second-century publications on Jesus share a common metanarrative consisting of three basic settings, like three acts of a drama. The first act is set in the invisible world of divine powers and results in the creation of the material world. The second act covers the activity of a Son of one of the divine powers who appears in human form on earth, delivers a message to humankind, and dies on the cross. The third act is set after the return of the Son to the Divine Power who sent him, and it shows how the Son's new status plays out in the spiritual experience of those who believed him and acted on the message he delivered to the world.

Although second- and third-century books on Jesus agree on these three settings of the plot, the genre allows for poetic license. The border between narrative traditions about Jesus and visionary experiences of Christ is fluid. Narrative perspectives reach from Christ telling his own story to disciples providing eyewitness accounts to first followers describing their visions to philosophers figuring out God's plan for the world.

Books are used as the central medium to communicate the Son's divine message to humankind in hopes that the written record transcends the lifespan of an individual and passes on knowledge from one generation to the next. This literary device delivers secret traditions, which had been written down a long time ago in the hand of enlightened eyewitnesses and were made accessible to the public for the first time. Readers are expected to be familiar with a culture of book production and, more specifically, to be able to distinguish between the ancient author and the contemporary publisher.

The publications typically use first-century voices to address second-century concerns. A popular strategy was to fill in gaps left open in the shared metanarrative. Narrative discrepancies are usually perceived as corrections to traditional accounts and boost the credibility of the most recent publication.

Dating Books on Jesus and His Early Followers

Some books, like Mary's gospel book, are dated because of the age of the oldest manuscript fragments. Others, like the *Gospel of Truth*, the anonymous Infancy gospel book attributed to Thomas, James's gospel book, and the Marcionite Edition, are dated because of perceived references to them in second-century writings. Books like *Invisible Spirit* or *Dialogue of the Savior* or *Second Discourse of Seth* that are found in the Nag-Hammadi codices of the fifth century are Coptic translations of earlier Greek writings. And because they cover topics documented for the second century, like the discussion of the Demiurge, the role of women in congregations, and the authority of Jewish Scripture for Christians, they are assigned to this period. All these categories— manuscript evidence, first documented readers, contemporary issues— are used to date the Canonical Edition as well.

Why Did People Write and Publish Books about Jesus?

It seems unlikely that Christ wrote about his adventures on earth and published *Second Discourse of Great Seth* after returning to heaven. But why would someone write such a book? And why would anyone want to read it?

Readers decide about the success of a publication, not publishers. If a publisher knew which book would sell, she or he would produce fewer titles and sell select books in higher numbers. Books pass the test of time only if they resonate with audiences. From a historian's perspective, a successfully distributed book conveys reliable information about the mindset of its historical readers, no matter how imaginative the content is.

Many second-century books on Jesus provide secret knowledge that promises to explain the otherwise unexplainable. Christian faith communities pass on wisdom from one generation to the next, transcending time and geographical boundaries. Who is better suited to explain the mystery of a god sending his Son to earth than Jesus himself? Gospel books typically create a platform to stage the speeches of Jesus and Christ, and historical reading communities were willing to buy such books. They wanted to hear what Jesus had to say and accepted the literary format in which the message, called "the good news," was presented.

"Truth" is experienced in the community of believers and endorsed by the leadership of a faith community. Authors and publishers will get away with any story if it resonates with their audience. So, the reasons for the production and survival of these books are the same reasons as for any other successful publication: they found and help make their audience.

IV

WHY IS THE CANONICAL EDITION A COLLECTION OF AUTOGRAPHS?

COMPARED WITH OTHER publications about Jesus and his followers, two characteristics stand out: first, the Canonical Edition is a collection and not a stand-alone book. The closest parallel in the surveyed examples is the Marcionite Edition. Whereas the Marcionite Edition speaks only with the voice of Paul, the Canonical Edition conveys its message through a variety of voices.

And second, the Canonical Edition contains autographs. The publisher indicates that in many cases the edition is based on originals written in the hand of the author who is mentioned in the title. For example, the publisher mentions a manuscript that was written by John himself that he used for Gospel according to John, 2 Thessalonians displayed Paul's signature, and the publisher used the manuscript that Luke had submitted to produce Gospel according to Luke and Acts of Apostles. The *Secret Book of John*, the *Secret Book of James*, and the *Infancy Gospel of James* use the same literary device: they are based on autographs and transmitted by trustworthy custodians.

To better understand the genre, the next section will look at historical examples of edited collections of autographs. Three examples are introduced to demonstrate typical characteristics: the fourteenth-century collection of Duke Rudolf IV of Austria, which included the Privilegium maius, the Lilienfeld Chronicles produced by Chrysostomus Hanthaler in the eighteenth century, and the infamous Hitler Diaries created by Konrad Kujau at the end of the twentieth century. These obscure collections are selected because they have nothing to do with biblical literature and because they originated in different centuries. The strength of form-critical assessments is that genres exist over long periods of time. Genres are like the body language of two persons, not identical but similar. Typical features of edited collections of autographs include the following: they serve a political agenda; authentication is more important than authenticity; they provide information from the past that impacts present conflicts; publishers are responsible for interpolations and additional writings and have often been identified; and larger collections usually replace shorter collections in the marketplace.

The survey is complemented by two well-researched edited collections of Christian materials, Julian's editions of apostolic documents and Letters of Ignatius published in the fourth century and the Pseudo-Isidorian Decretals of the ninth century.

These explorations may feel awkward and unexpected in a book about the origins of Christian Scripture, but it would not be the first time in the history of interpretation that form-critical insights throw fresh light on an old set of questions.

§6
Diverse Examples

Apostolic Constitutions and Letters of Ignatius

Two Christian publications, the *Apostolic Constitutions* and an enlarged and interpolated edition of letters by Bishop Ignatius of Antioch, offer an example of how scholars successfully dated the first editions of two edited collections. The result was that the same person, a certain Julian, who also authored a commentary on Job, created both collections. He lived during the second half of the fourth century.[1]

Apostolic Constitutions
The *Apostolic Constitutions* regulate communal life and contain instructions for clergy and laypeople. The editorial narrative presents the work as the teachings of the twelve apostles in eight volumes, published by a certain Clement.[2]

As far as the literary technique is concerned, the editor mixed traditional material with fictional texts. Because several writings have survived independently, it is possible to recognize the interpolations and describe the editorial changes. The *Didascalia Apostolorum,* which survived in a Syriac and in part in a Latin translation of the Greek, was used for the first six books. The first half of the seventh book is based on the *Didache,* and the eighth book follows the *Apostolic Constitution* by Hippolytus. Not all texts used for the remainder of this collection can be identified with certainty.[3] But despite the disparate character of the individual writings, the *Apostolic Constitutions* are presented to the readers as one work in eight volumes.

At the end of this collection, as part of the eighty-fifth canon, the books of the New Testament are listed. Between the Catholic Letters and Acts, the implied publisher, Clement, endorses his own work, the Apostolic "Constitutions."[4]

> *But our sacred books, that is, those of the New Testament, are these: the four Gospels of Matthew, Mark, Luke, and John; the fourteen Letters of Paul; two Letters of Peter, three of John, one of James, one of Jude; two Letters of Clement; and the* Constitutions *dedicated to you the bishops by me* Clement, *in eight books; to publish the Constitutions for everyone is not appropriate,* because of the mysteries they contain; *and the Acts of us the Apostles. (ApostConst 8:47 canon 85)*

First historical readers who wondered why they had not heard about the Apostolic Constitutions receive an explanation: the writings had not been published before "because of the mysteries they contain."

Letters of Ignatius

According to his letters, Ignatius was Bishop of Antioch during the first half of the second century. The manuscript tradition is dominated by an edition that inserted passages into seven previously published letters and added six more to the collection.[5] Because the earlier edition survived, the editorial changes are easily identified. The technique to interpolate the traditional text and add new material is like the technique used for the Apostolic Constitutions, and because both collections also show similar repetitive expressions and parallels, the scholarly consensus suggested that the same person edited both works. But only recently has this person been identified.[6]

In 1973, Dieter Hagedorn, professor of papyrology at the University of Heidelberg, published a commentary on Job, known from four Greek manuscripts.[7] As he was trying to understand peculiar theological statements and concepts, he regularly came across parallels in the Apostolic Constitutions. He then realized that characteristic elements of style matched as well, and it soon became clear to him that he was looking at a publication that was almost certainly authored by the same person who had created the Apostolic Constitutions and the enlarged edition of the Letters of Ignatius.[8] The commentary on Job, however, was not anonymous; the manuscript and catena tradition ascribe this work to a certain Julian.

Once the person was identified, the place and date of the first edition of the Apostolic Constitutions and the enlarged edition of the Letters of Ignatius could be determined. Hagedorn concluded that Julian prepared these collections for publication between 350 and 380; he probably came from Syria and was a follower of Arius.[9]

Identifying the Publisher

Because earlier versions of many individual writings survived, the editorial changes were easily identified. The focus on the editorial narrative, instead of on the authors of the individual writings, allowed for an identification of the person who had edited the *Apostolic Constitutions* and the expanded edition of the *Letters of Ignatius*, and for a determination of the place and date of the first edition.

Other characteristics of edited collections of documents are: the high number of writings collected, the blatant self-endorsement of the collection through the voice of the implied publisher, and the well-documented political impact of the Arian Controversy on the Catholic community.

The *Pseudo-Isidorian Decretals*

In the middle of the ninth century, a large collection of canons of the Catholic Church was introduced in lawsuits between Western Frankish bishops and their superiors, the archbishops and provincial synods.[10] The collection is referred to as the *Pseudo-Isidorian Decretals* and contains mostly canons of the synods and councils and papal letters, reaching from first-century Bishop Clement of Rome to Pope Gregory II (715–731), whose Council of 721 provides the final document.[11] So, roughly a century has passed between the implied date of the collection, 721, and its first appearance in the lawsuits of the ninth century. It is estimated that the collection pieced together more than ten thousand excerpts from previously published collections.[12]

According to the documents collected in Pseudo-Isidore, accusations against bishops were no longer to be decided by provincial and national synods but had to be handled by the pope, who alone had the right to confirm the decisions of the councils.[13]

The implied publisher calls himself Isidore Mercator, which is reflected in the scholarly designation Pseudo-Isidore.[14] The name seems to conflate Isidore of Seville, a bishop and important scholar of the Early Middle Ages, and Marius Mercator, an ecclesiastical writer of the fifth century.[15]

The strategy of the Decretals was to create credibility by overwhelming readers with many seemingly independent documents that were issued by different authors under diverse circumstances. Fictional documents were usually created from citations of traditional material. The number of mosaic-like excerpts easily exceeds ten thousand.[16] The main interest of all these ordinances was to protect the ecclesiastical authority of the bishops by emphasizing among other measures their traditional right to appeal to the pope.[17]

When the Decretals were introduced in the West-Frankish cleric trials, however, they were met with skepticism. Archbishop Hinkmar of Reims recognized the potentially fictitious character of some of the documents and inquired in Rome as to whether the originals existed in the archives.[18] Pope Nicholas I, who liked the message of the Decretals, authenticated them.[19]

Significant progress in identifying the historical editor of the corpus has been made only very recently.[20] Once the West-Frankish cleric trials were identified as the conflict that the Pseudo-Isidorian Decretals addressed, their publication could be dated more precisely to the second half of the ninth century, and the monasteries where they were produced and some individuals who edited and published the collection can now be identified.[21]

Information from the Past Impacting Present Conflicts

The editorial narrative addresses a significant conflict at the time of publication, just as the editions published by Julian, Rudolph IV, and Hanthaler did. Past events are imagined but the impact of this revisionist activity is real and can be described using historical methodology. The *Pseudo-Isidorian Decretals* are also an example of publishers heavily interpolating traditional writings and adding fictitious documents.

Privilegium Maius

The House of Habsburg occupied the throne of the Holy Roman Empire from 1440 until its dissolution in 1806. Their claim to be eligible for the throne is based on the *Privilegium maius*, a document of controversial provenance. The original is kept at the State Archives of Austria.

In 1360, Emperor Charles IV asked Francesco Petrarch, the celebrated humanist and renaissance scholar, for his scholarly opinion on the authenticity of letters by Caesar and Nero, which were quoted in a collection of documents that his son-in-law, Rudolph IV of Austria, had supposedly discovered in the family archives.[22] The central document of the collection, the so-called *Privilegium maius*, purported to have been issued by King Henry IV in 1058, three hundred years earlier.[23]

Petrarch suspected the letters of Caesar and Nero to be forgeries, and Emperor Charles IV refused to confirm the authenticity of the collection, including the Privilegium maius. However, when the Austrian regent Frederick V became Holy Roman Emperor Frederick III in 1452, the Privilegium maius was declared authentic. It remained a relevant legal document until the dissolution of the Holy Roman Empire in 1806.

In 1852 the Berlin scholar Wilhelm Wattenbach studied the Privilegium maius in the context of the five documents among which it was presented and established that the Privilegium maius was a forgery.[24]

The first document of the collection was issued by King Heinrich IV in 1058. It confirmed privileges given to Austria by the Roman emperors Julius Caesar and Nero, whose letters were quoted in full. Heinrich IV's endorsement made those letters legally relevant.

The second document was the Privilegium maius proper, which granted the House of Habsburg the status of prince-electors. It was recorded on the same day as the Privilegium minus in 1156 by Emperor Friedrich I.[25]

The third document was issued by King Henry VII in 1228 and provided privileges about acquiring other countries without permission by the emperor. The regulations were extraordinarily detailed.[26]

The fourth document, issued by Emperor Friedrich II in 1245, confirmed the Privilegium maius and added more privileges.[27]

The fifth document authenticated the first four documents, expressly referring to the letters of Julius Caesar and Nero. It was issued by King Rudolph IV in the presence of the prince-electors in 1283.[28] The individual documents were referred to by date and issuing authority. By numbering the five documents and arranging them chronologically, an editorial frame was created that supported the editorial narrative. They ceased being individual documents and became part of an edited collection.

Although the authenticity of the collection was rejected by Emperor Charles IV when it first surfaced, the authenticity was upheld a century later when the privileges were endorsed by Emperor Friedrich III in 1453 and confirmed by Charles V in 1530, by Rudolph II in 1699, and by Charles VI in 1729.[29] Charles V even passed an ordinance that prevented the courts from gaining access to the originals and forbade anyone to engage in a critical discussion of their authenticity.[30]

Wattenbach assumed that the Privilegium maius was the important document and that the other documents only served as support, like a padded envelope protects a delicate item. He therefore ignored the question of authenticity and instead concentrated on the significance this edited collection held for the publisher, Duke Rudolph IV, and its first documented historical reader, Emperor Charles IV.

He reconstructed the historical situation under Duke Rudolph IV in the following way.[31] Albrecht II, father of Rudolph IV, had negotiated Rudolph's marriage with a daughter of Emperor Charles IV. And because the emperor had no sons, Albrecht hoped that his son Rudolph would one day succeed Charles and become emperor. The two men may have even made a secret arrangement to secure this promise. Unfortunately for Rudolph, he was only nineteen years old when his father died. The same year, the emperor's third wife became pregnant with a daughter and renewed the emperor's hopes to father a son. In addition to this development, which must have been experienced by Rudolph as a catastrophe, Emperor Charles IV had, only four years earlier in 1356, issued the Golden Bull, which named the seven prince-electors who participated in the election of the emperor of the Holy Roman Empire. The House of Habsburg was not one of them. The Privilegium maius, however, would have elevated the status of Habsburg rulers to prince-electors. But this was no longer in the interests of Emperor Charles IV, who now wanted to secure the throne for someone in his own lineage.

If this historical assessment is correct, it provides an explanation for why, in the fourteenth century, Emperor Charles IV was not interested in endorsing the editorial narrative of Rudolph's collection.[32] It is also easily understood why, in the fifteenth century, Friedrich III, the first emperor from the House of Habsburg, liked the editorial narrative and declared the Privilegium maius authentic and why, in the sixteenth century, the Habsburg Emperor Charles V did not allow anyone to investigate the authenticity of the documents.[33]

Authentication and Authenticity
The example demonstrates that, in a political setting, authentication matters more than authenticity. Francesco Petrarch's reservations as to whether Julius Caesar and Emperor Nero really wrote the letters included in the collection became irrelevant as soon as a king endorsed or denounced them. The term *political* in this context means that the well-being of the community, represented by its governing authority, outweighs the concern for authenticity.[34]

Lilienfeld Chronicles

Another corpus that influenced historians of the House of Habsburg was first published by Chrysostomus Hanthaler (1690–1754), librarian of the Lower-Austrian Lilienfeld Abbey. It presented documents from the eleventh to the thirteenth century.[35]

In 1742, Chrysostomus Hanthaler made the public aware of a recently discovered manuscript written by a certain Ortilo. Ortilo was a monk who had been ordered by Herzog Leopold VI to move to Lilienfeld and found the monastery, where Hanthaler was working as the librarian.

Five years later, in 1747, Hanthaler published a history of the monastery, the *Fasti Campililiensis (Lilienfeld Chronicles)*, using Ortilo and two additional sources.[36] One was a manuscript by the Dominican Alold of Pöchlarn, chaplain of Herzog Leopold VI (died 1055), who had kept a record of significant events from the early Austrian history until 1198. The other source was by Leupold von Lilienfeld, a monk at the monastery since 1330, who copied an otherwise undocumented older chronicle.[37]

Unfortunately, the manuscripts by Alold and Leupold were mostly destroyed in a fire, but a few samples survived.[38] When they were inspected 150 years after Hanthaler's death, it turned out that the handwriting of Leupold from 1355 was identical with the handwriting of Ortilo from 1230. The compelling conclusion was that Hanthaler had fabricated both.[39]

Hanthaler's strategy was to let the sources speak for themselves and to present his own voice as a commentary that may or may not be correct. Critics had been skeptical of the historical value of Hanthaler's sources, but they still commended Hanthaler on his discovery.[40] They reasoned that even if these documents were not authentic, it was not Hanthaler's fault. He had only discovered them. No one suspected that the publisher had also fabricated his sources.

The strategy to present himself as the discoverer and publisher shielded Hanthaler from being exposed during his lifetime. It also misled students of the early history of the House of Habsburg for centuries.[41]

Why were the Lilienfeld Chronicles relevant to the public?

Almost six hundred years before Hanthaler published the chronicles, in 1142, the Babenberg Heinrich II married an Austrian lady by the name of Gertrud.[42] She died within a year. An inscription kept the memory alive, but the connection to Heinrich II was eventually forgotten. There is also a trustworthy source indicating that Herzog Friedrich II was married in Braunschweig in 1226, but it was unclear whom he married. The official narrative of the Austrian rulers conflated these traditions and presented Gertrud as a noblewoman from Braunschweig and made her the first wife of Friedrich II, who soon abandoned her and married Agnes von Meran. The story was of public interest at the time of Hanthaler because of the parallels to the marriage of Charles VI with another noblewoman of Braunschweig-Lüneburg, Elisabeth Christine. Their union had not yet produced offspring.[43]

In 1716, J. G. Eckard, a contemporary of Hanthaler, published a historical-critical study that challenged the validity of the official genealogy of the Austrian rulers. Eckard argued that there was no woman on record from the house of Braunschweig who could have married Friedrich II, certainly no one by the name of Gertrud. He also was able to demonstrate that Heinrich's first wife was a Greek princess, the sister of the wife of Belas IV of Hungary.

Hanthaler came to the rescue of the official tradition. He did this by interpolating the historical register of the monastery (Lilienfelder Totenbuch) and adding passages in his own hand. He also provided detailed information through Ortilo and Pernold, presumed autographic manuscripts, sources Hanthaler had fabricated himself. They indicated that Heinrich was married three times, first to Gertrud, then to the Greek princess by the otherwise undocumented name Sophie, and finally to Agnes von Meran.

Again, Hanthaler's strategy was to introduce autographs, which supported the traditional narrative by offering otherwise undocumented information. The historian's argument, put forward by Eckard, was based on the argument of silence, but Hanthaler's solution was based on a source. And when an audience is offered the choice to either not know at all or to discuss a dubious source, they almost always prefer to follow the source. The story of Heinrich's three wives is one of many examples that shed light on Hanthaler's method.

Publishers Interpolate and Enlarge Collections

Although publishers usually are seen as trustworthy professionals who pass on what they received unchanged, the example of the *Lilienfeld Chronicles* illustrates that publishers are not always to be trusted. If they choose to, they may interpolate traditional documents and produce additional writings. Rudolph IV had done the same with his collection.

Hitler Diaries

On April 22, 1983, the German news magazine *Stern* published excerpts of diaries written by Adolf Hitler in his own hand. Hugh Trevor-Roper (Lord Dacre, 1914–2003) was one of the experts who had authenticated the diaries. A scholar with a stellar academic career, he was also known outside of academia through his book, *The Last Days of Hitler*.[44]

The Times, who had hired Trevor-Roper as an expert, asked him to sign a nondisclosure agreement. He was given brief access to the originals and asked to immediately make a statement. This statement was heavily edited to sensationalize the discovery. The sixty volumes contained an enormous amount of insignificant detail, which indicated to the seasoned historian that the volumes were authentic. He felt that a forger would not have needed to go to such lengths just to promote a few statements that were relevant to his or her agenda.

Trevor-Roper's contractual agreement to not confer with external experts turned out to be unfortunate because he was well acquainted with the historian Eberhard Jäckel, who had his own painful experiences with similar documents. Trevor-Roper's skepticism grew when he visited with Gerd Heidemann, the journalist who had presented the diaries to *Stern*. In his apartment, Heidemann showed the astonished scholar hundreds of folders of documents, plus some four hundred drawings and watercolors, apparently rescued from the wrecked plane that had also carried the diaries. The Hitler Diaries were part of a much larger discovery of autographs.

But how could a critical historian like Trevor-Roper so easily be misled? Trevor-Roper explained later that he had put too much confidence in the expertise *Stern* had presented. Three independent experts had declared the handwriting to be authentic. The editors of the magazine assured him that the German military officer who had secured the material from the plane's wreckage in 1945 was still alive but preferred to stay anonymous.

The debate ended abruptly when the forensic analysis of the ink suggested a date after Hitler's death in 1945, and the journalist Gerd Heidemann admitted that the mysterious Wehrmachtsoffizier did not exist. He had made up the story to create plausibility. And when Konrad Kujau, the dealer who had provided the diaries as well as the forged Hitler autographs used by the experts to authenticate the handwriting, confessed that he had written the sixty volumes himself, the matter was settled.

The *Sunday Times* gave up their plans to publish the Hitler Diaries in a serialized format and instead issued an official apology. They felt that promoting fictitious writings as authentic documents violated professional standards of journalism. The German *Stern* magazine felt compromised. The staff involved resigned.

A Large Collection Creates Credibility
The fact that the collection was so large threw Trevor-Roper's judgment. Sixty volumes, which often covered trivial events of the day and were preserved in autographs, created the impression of authentic documents. Historians would be ill-advised to use the size of a collection of autographs as an argument for authenticity.

§7
Shared Features

Publishers Authenticate

Authentication makes a document relevant to the community, not authenticity. The letters of Nero and Caesar became legally relevant when they were authenticated by Rudolph IV and later by the Habsburg emperors. Their voices told the story the way the Habsburg rulers wanted it to be heard. Pope Nicolaus authenticated Isidore Mercator's collection because he supported the message, not because he had seen the autographs.

When a publisher presents an autograph, the publisher becomes the authenticator. Readers do not have access to the originals; they only have access to published copies through the lens of the editorial narrative. Rudolph IV guaranteed the authenticity of the Privilegium maius, Hanthaler offered handwritten chronicles, and *Stern* published transcripts of diaries penned by Hitler. In each case the publisher stood for the authenticity of the autographs.

Self-endorsements

The fifth document of Rudolph IV's collection authenticated the first four documents in the presence of the prince-electors. In the Apostolic Constitutions, the editor, Clement, presumably the legendary Bishop of Rome, had his collection endorsed by the apostles.

At first sight having a collection authenticate itself seems an unpersuasive strategy. Nevertheless, it is quite common, specifically for collections of fictitious documents. Signs of authenticity like autographic subscriptions, signatures, or seals are clearly visible on the original and need no further mentioning. They are, however, missing in a transcript. So, comments like, "This is my handwriting, it is the sign of authenticity," are not necessary in the original because every reader will easily recognize the change of hands. But they are essential signals for a publisher of spurious writings. Self-endorsements and excessive claims of authenticity should raise skepticism.

The Latest Edition Carries the Most Authority

If two edited collections of the same materials exist, the larger one is usually the most recent one.

Although edited collections of documents typically enlarge other published collections, they present themselves closer to the original than the collections they enlarge. The suggestion is that the collection improves its historical accuracy through editing. Ironically, the most recent critical edition of an ancient author is perceived in the market as presenting the best text. This phenomenon has helped Julian, Pseudo-Isidore, and Rudolph IV to promote their publications.

Twin Forgeries

The strategy of producing twin forgeries, where one fictitious document proves the authenticity of the other one, is obvious in Hanthaler's collections, where the two handwritten sources of Alold and Leupold were both written in Hanthaler's hand and supported each other's credibility.

Once Konrad Kujau admitted that he had fabricated the Hitler Diaries, his strategy to deceive readers about the true authorship became evident. He had produced Hitler's diaries as well as the autographs that the experts used to authentic the hand. The experts' judgment was correct; the hands were identical. Their conclusion, however, that Hitler wrote the diaries, was faulty.

Repeated themes in otherwise dissimilar writings collected in the Apostolic Constitutions and in the enlarged edition of the Letters of Ignatius are so evident that it gave away the identity of the editor, Julian. In a similar manner, the repetitive messaging in seemingly independent documents allowed scholars to recognize and date the historical interpolators and publishers of the Pseudo-Isidorian Decretals.

Editorial Narratives Are Not Historically Reliable

Like all stories, the editorial narrative of a collection of autographs allows for poetic license. It is the result of a creative process. Collections that claim to edit historical documents for publication but include fictitious documents have no reservations to interpolate traditional writings, spin the message, and display a revisionist attitude toward generally accepted historical events.

Historians often debunk the credibility of an editorial narrative by investigating the authors and discovering discrepancies and anachronisms: Ignatius did not support the Christological concepts of Arian, Hitler suffered from a medical condition that did not allow him to write with his own hand, Gaius Caesar did not support the House of Habsburg, and Isidore of Seville did not think that bishops should be above the law of their governments. Therefore, they could hardly be the authors of the documents issued in their name.

Nevertheless, editorial narratives are not without historical merit. They express opinions about past events held by publishers, editors, and readers at the time of publication, just as science-fiction novels do about future events. Jules Verne's writings, for example, provide reliable historical information about scientific theories during the second half of the nineteenth century, when they were published.

Whereas the creative and engaging nature of the editorial narrative must be honored, the storyline, however, should not be taken as a reliable representation of historical events.

Delayed Impact

Edited collections of documents show a strong interest in influencing a community by using a voice from the past to speak to contemporary issues. And sometimes they exert their full political potential long after their first publication. Isidore's ninth-century Decretals set the stage for the Investiture Controversy of the eleventh and twelfth centuries. Rudolph IV provided the legal basis for the Habsburg rulers to become emperors of the Roman Empire eighty-seven years after his death.

§8
Implications of Understanding the Canonical Edition as an Edited Collection of Autographs

Priority of the Marcionite Edition

Early adopters of the Canonical Edition experienced the Marcionite Edition as a redacted version of the Canonical Edition. And because the editions share eleven writings, the relationship between the Canonical Edition and the Marcionite Edition is a literary dependency. They did not originate independently from each other without one knowing about the other. However, the study of edited collections of autographs suggests that more extended editions of the same material usually interpolate traditional documents and add writings to the shorter edition.

Therefore, it is much more likely that the Marcionite Edition served as the template for the Canonical Edition than the other way around. The Canonical Edition interpolated the text of the Marcionite Edition and added writings to it.

Consistent with the observation that the longer collection succeeds in the marketplace, the number of twenty-seven first-century writings included in the Canonical Edition is quite staggering—more than double the eleven writings the Marcionite Edition had to offer.

The Canonical Edition reflects the culture of other second-century books on Jesus, which assume that early followers of Jesus wrote down their experiences a hundred years earlier and that these manuscripts were miraculously preserved and published for the first time. Characters of the Jesus story like John, Peter, Paul, Mary, Philip, Levi, Matthew, Jude, and Thomas are popular characters in other Christian publications as well. And the belief that the Invisible God sent a "Son" from heaven down into "the world" to open the eyes of those who listened and believed so that they could overcome death and enjoy "eternal life" is shared with many second- and third-century publications.[45]

The idea that there was only one God in heaven, the creator of the material world, and that he only had one Son, differentiated the faith community that endorsed the Canonical Edition from other Christian communities in the second century.

Identifying the Implied Publisher of the Canonical Edition

Edited collections combine three voices: the author's voice, the publisher's voice, and the editor's voice.[46] The author submits a manuscript, the publisher sponsors it, and then editors prepare the manuscript for publication. One person can combine two or all three functions, but distinguishing between publisher, editor, and author helps separate the interwoven narratives.

Historical publishers, who interpolate and enlarge traditional collections, may use the voice of an implied publisher to promote their views. For example, the implied publisher of the Pseudo-Isidorian Decretals introduced himself with the following words.[47]

> *Isidor Mercator, servant of Christ, to the reader, his fellow-servant and believer in the Lord, greetings. I was ordered by many bishops and other servants of God* to collect and edit *into one volume the summaries (sententiae) of the canons and* to make out of many one. *However, I found this very difficult because the* different interpretations had produced *different summaries. And although there can only be one meaning, the summaries nevertheless show* variations, *some* are longer, and others are shorter.

Isidor Mercator addressed the reader as he talked about the documents that he was asked "to collect and edit." Because he speaks in the first-person singular, it becomes possible to discern between the voice of the publisher and the authorial voice of the documents.[48] Furthermore, the publisher discloses an editorial process: the individual documents are taken from different sources, edited for consistency, and combined into one literary work "to make out of many one." He specifically points out that in the surveyed manuscripts, some copies of the same document "are longer, and others are shorter," rather bluntly preparing readers, who were familiar with the traditional writings, for the numerous interpolations.[49]

So, who is the implied publisher of the Canonical Edition?

In the last sentence of Gospel according to John, the implied publisher addressed readers as if they already knew him.

> *But there are also* many other *things that Jesus did; if every one of them were written down,* I suppose *that the world itself could not contain the* books *that would be written. (John 21:25)*

By switching to the first-person singular ("I suppose"), the publisher distinguishes his own voice from the voice of the authors Matthew, Mark, Luke, John, and the voice of competing publications ("books").

So, if the publisher assumes that readers know him, where was he introduced?

The only passage in the Four-Gospel volume that identifies a publisher by name is in Luke's introduction to his gospel book and to his book on the apostles. Luke dedicated both volumes to a "most excellent Theophilus."

> *I too decided, after investigating everything carefully from the very first, to write an orderly account for you,* most excellent Theophilus, *so that you may know the truth concerning the things about which you have been instructed. (Luke 1:3–4)*

> *In the first book,* Theophilus, *I wrote about all that Jesus did and taught from the beginning until the day when he was taken up to heaven. (Acts 1:1–2)*

Dedications at the beginning of books indicated the sponsor and potential publisher who was asked to safeguard the author's manuscript, oversee the final editing, and produce the work in sufficient numbers for distribution.[50] Theophilus is the only person in the New Testament who is introduced to readers as a publisher.

Consequently, and for lack of an alternative, a literary approach must conclude that it is Theophilus who speaks with his own voice at the end of the Four-Gospel volume, the person who published Luke's writings. And because Acts of Apostles is part of the Praxapostolos volume, Theophilus is not just the publisher of the Four-Gospel volume but also the publisher of the Praxapostolos volume, and because these two volumes cannot be separated from the Fourteen-Letters-of-Paul volume and Revelation of John, he becomes the publisher of the Canonical Edition.

Staying within the narrative world of the Canonical Edition, from this point on, Theophilus will be treated as the name of the implied publisher.

V

THE DESIGN OF THE CANONICAL EDITION

THE FOLLOWING SECTION will explore the New Testament as an interpolated and enlarged publication of the late second century, which was
produced for an international Greek-speaking readership in Central
Europe, North Africa, Asia Minor, and Greece. It is assumed that the
historical editors interpolated and enlarged the Marcionite Edition. It
is also assumed that they presented the interpolated and added documents as authentic.

The survey of comparable publications suggests that historical
publishers, who authorize interpolations and add writings, use the
voice of the implied publishers to promote their own views. Consequently, the voice of the implied publisher, expressed in the editorial
narrative of the Canonical Edition, communicates the message of the
historical publisher. When, however, an existing collection is interpolated and enlarged with fictional documents, an element of poetic
license is introduced. And readers are well advised not to take the setting, characters, conflict, and plot of the editorial narrative as historical
information.

The editorial narrative of the Canonical Edition names a certain Theophilus as the implied publisher. Luke dedicates two books to
Theophilus. Theophilus adds the gospel books by Matthew and Mark
to Luke's first book and the letters of James, Peter, and Jude to Luke's
second book. He completes the collection by including fourteen letters of Paul and five writings of John. Theophilus organizes this material in four volumes: the Four-Gospel volume, the Praxapostolos, the
Fourteen-Letters-of-Paul volume, and Revelation of John.

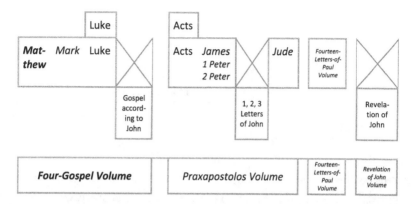

The editorial narrative reaches a point in time when Paul is in Rome and faces his day in court.[1] This was the implied date when Theophilus published the Canonical Edition.[2]

The following section is an exercise in listening to the implied publisher, Theophilus, in his attempt "to make out of many one," as he includes the writings of John and produces the Canonical Edition of the New Testament.

§9
Theophilus and the Writings of John

The Canonical Edition interpolated eleven writings and added sixteen new ones to the Marcionite Edition. Of these additional writings, John is the most prominent author, with five books: a gospel book, three letters, and Revelation of John.

Second-century publications on Jesus assumed that readers were familiar with the basic process of preparing manuscripts for publication, specifically that they were able to distinguish between publisher, editors, and author.[3] This insight is helpful for the interpretation of the writings of John.

Gospel According to John

Gospel according to John speaks with four voices: the voice of the editors, author, Spirit, and publisher.

Voice of the Editors

As the editors prepare John's manuscript for publication, they distinguish between their own voice and the voice of the disciple. "This is *the disciple* who is testifying to these things and has written them, and *we know* that *his testimony* is true."[4]

And when they quote John's manuscript for the last time, they report a conversation between Jesus and Peter. In the eyes of the editors, some had misinterpreted what the author wanted to say.

> *Peter turned and saw the disciple whom Jesus loved*
> *following them.*

*1 He was the one who had reclined next to Jesus at the supper and had said, "Lord, who is it that is going to betray you?"

> *When Peter saw him, he said to Jesus, "Lord, what about*
> *him?" Jesus said to him, "If it is my will that he remain until*
> *I come, what is that to you? Follow me!"*

*2 So, the rumor spread in the community that this disciple would not die. Yet Jesus did not say to him that he would not die, but "If it is my will that he remain until I come, what is that to you?" This is the disciple who is testifying to these things and has written them, and we know that his testimony is true.

In their first remark, the editors clarify that the "disciple whom Jesus loved" had been mentioned earlier in John's manuscript, and they identify the passage by quoting from it.[5] Cross-referencing characters in the manuscript of John is a strategy the editors also use for Lazarus and Caiaphas.[6] And when it comes to Judas, they make sure readers do not confuse him with another disciple of the same name by adding that this Judas is "the one who was about to betray him."[7]

In their second remark, the editors quote, "If it is my will that he remain until I come, what is that to you?" Quoting is as precise a reference as a footnote reference mark in a modern critical edition. The editors argue that a close reading of the quote from John's manuscript fails to support the contemporary opinion that Jesus had promised to return during the lifetime of John.[8]

Clearly, it is expected that attentive readers recognize where the voice of the editors begins and ends. To name a few signals even readers of translations can pick up: the voice of the editors is recognizable when they shift from the voice of the author to talking about the author, when they shift away from the place and time of Jesus to address the readers, or when they shift to the first-person plural "we."[9] Most modern translations do not separate between the text of John's manuscript and the editorial notes, and some translations put the editorial asides in parentheses.[10]

One group of editorial comments translated Aramaic or Hebrew words into Greek. When, for example, John's manuscript presents a dialogue, and the person says "Rabbi," the editors interrupt the dialogue and explain to the reader, "Which translated means Teacher"; or when someone uses the word "Messiah," they explain, "Which is translated Anointed"; or when "Cephas" appears in John's manuscript they add "Which is translated, Peter."[11] If such a dialogue were read out loud, the performer would have to turn to the audience, give the explanation in his own voice, and then slip back into the voice of the character in the dialogue.

Other remarks provide information from outside the text, like, "It was not Jesus himself but his disciples who baptized"; or they clarify something that is presupposed but not expressly said in John's manuscript, like, "His disciples had gone to the city to buy food"; or they explain the cultural background like, "Jews do not share things in common with Samaritans."[12]

Since the editors talked about themselves in first-person plural when they wrote "we know that his testimony is true" (John 21:24) at the end of the book, readers may suspect an editorial comment each time they come across a passage written in first-person plural that interrupts the flow. In the dialogue between Nicodemus and Jesus,

Nicodemus asks, "How can these things be?" and Jesus answers, "Are you a teacher of Israel, and yet you do not understand these things? Very truly, I tell you. . . . " At this point, the dialogue is interrupted, and the editors comment in their own voices, "We speak of what we know and testify to what we have seen; yet you do not receive our testimony." And Jesus continues the sentence in the first-person again, "If I talk to you about earthly things and you do not believe, how can you believe if I talk to you about heavenly things?" And when this dialogue comes to an end, the editors add a lengthy commentary that begins with the statement, "No one has ascended into heaven except the one who descended from heaven." Jesus is not talking anymore; the editors are talking about Jesus.[13] When readers are encouraged to discern between the manuscript of the Beloved Disciple and editorial explanations, they will recognize such general expositions as editorial comments.

And finally, there is a group of most fascinating editorial remarks that reference content from the three preceding gospels of Matthew, Mark, and Luke. These editorial remarks assume that readers of the fourth gospel book are familiar with the three preceding books of the Four-Gospel volume. They are written from the perspective of Theophilus, the implied publisher of the Canonical Edition.

When the narrative first mentions the name "John," it is with the words "There was a man sent from God, whose name was John."[14] If Gospel according to John is the only book about Jesus that readers are aware of, they would have to think that this is the John mentioned in the title. But the following text clarifies that this is not John the Beloved Disciple and author of the manuscript but John the Baptist, a character who is prominently featured in the preceding gospels and, therefore, from the point of view of Theophilus, needs no introduction.[15]

When Lazarus is introduced, he is introduced by associating him with Mary and Martha: "Now a certain man was ill, Lazarus of Bethany, the village of Mary and her sister Martha."[16] Mary and Martha had not been mentioned before in Gospel according to John, yet readers are expected to know them. Mary and Martha are characters in Luke's account.[17]

By adding notes instead of simply changing the wording, the editors show respect for John's manuscript. They want to be appreciated as commentators, not as authors.

Voice of John

John's manuscript, the source that the editors are so carefully preparing for publication, displays a critical distance to Gospel according to Luke. At least twice, John corrects details of a story that is included in Luke, and that is missing in Matthew's and Mark's accounts: the story of the woman anointing Jesus's feet and the story of the miraculous catch of fish.

In Luke's account, the anointing happens during the Galilean period of Jesus's ministry, but John insists that the event occurred six days before Jesus's death. And it did not take place in the home of a Pharisee, as Luke will have it, but at the home of Lazarus in Bethany, just outside of Jerusalem. And most strikingly, the woman who anointed Jesus was not "a woman in the city who was a sinner," but according to John, it was Mary, the sister of Lazarus and Martha.[18]

And when it comes to the story of the miraculous catch of fish, John offers two major corrections to Luke's account. First, the timing is wrong. The event did not take place early in Jesus's ministry but happened after Jesus's resurrection. And in addition to the disciples Simon, James, and John, who are mentioned by Luke, four more eyewitnesses were present, "Thomas called the Twin, Nathanael of Cana in Galilee, and two others of his disciples."[19]

John also disagrees with Luke and sides with Matthew and Mark when it comes to the events following Easter Sunday. Mark foreshadows an appearance of Jesus in Galilee, and Matthew even delivers an account of this event.[20] According to Luke's gospel book, however, the resurrected Jesus never appeared in Galilee and ascended to heaven from Jerusalem on Easter Sunday.[21] John's manuscript insists that the resurrected Jesus showed himself to the disciples two additional times, one week after Easter in Jerusalem and later when they were fishing in Galilee.[22]

Voice of the Spirit

Gospel according to John offers speeches by Jesus that are too long to be understood as part of a dialogue.

The first of these monologues is loosely connected to a discussion between Jesus and the "Jews" about Jesus's healing a man on the Sabbath.[23] The following section is introduced with "Jesus said to them" and constitutes a lengthy monologue, which neither fits the stories in John's manuscript nor is editorial commentary. The monologue is only very superficially connected to the narrative. If this speech were removed, readers would not miss it. It abandons the setting in first-century Jerusalem and addresses timeless theological topics like resurrection from the dead, God's final judgment, the impending end of the world, the significance of John the Baptist, the authority of Jewish scriptures, the definition of true life, and the relevance of the law of Moses for humanity.[24]

The longest monologue in Gospel according to John spans four chapters (John 14–17), often called Jesus's farewell speeches. Jesus seems to talk directly to the readers. Toward the middle of the speech, Jesus says that God will continue to speak to them even after he returned to his heavenly Father, through the "Spirit of truth" and prepare them for "the things that are to come." This is a good definition of the monologues of Jesus in Gospel according to John. Jesus channels what he hears from the Spirit. And the disciples, like John, receive the promise that the Spirit will talk to them once Jesus has returned to his Father. Readers are to understand these passages as something that John wrote down as he was listening to the Spirit, who spoke using the voice of Jesus.[25]

> *I (Jesus) still have many things to say to you, but you cannot*
> *bear them now. When the* Spirit of truth *comes, he will*
> *guide you into all the truth; for he will not speak on his own,*

> *but will speak whatever he hears, and he will declare to you*
> the things that are to come. *(John 16:12–13)*

The literary strategy of providing monologues of Jesus as oracles of God interspersed between stories of Jesus finds ample parallels in second-century Christian literature. The *Secret Book of James*, the *Gospel of Mary*, the *Secret Book of John*, the *Gospel of Judas*, and the *Gospel of Thomas* are good examples. Jesus's monologues are loosely connected to the narrative setting. Questions from dialogue partners only prompt another speech, suggesting that the resurrected Christ is speaking to a second-century audience and not to the characters in the story.

From a literary point of view, the monologues are presented as taken from John's manuscript. The Beloved Disciple, like Mary Magdalene in her gospel book, received these speeches of Jesus as oracles of God through the Spirit and wrote them down.

Voice of the Implied Publisher

The implied publisher, Theophilus, introduces the Gospel according to John with a thoughtful meditation on the creation story in Genesis.[26] The divine Father of Jesus created everything through speech. He said, "Let there be light," and light came into existence. Therefore, Theophilus concludes that God created light and life through His word.[27] As the spoken word is immaterial and yet can be heard, it fits the concept of Christ as an immaterial Spirit who is sent into the material world by the Creator.

Because John the Baptist had already been introduced to readers of his Four-Gospel volume, Theophilus only reminds them of John's role in the editorial narrative of the New Testament: John the Baptist "was not the light, but he came to testify to the light."[28]

Then Theophilus returns to his meditation. If Jesus is the word of the Creator, then he also participated in the creation of the world. This statement is in accordance with other second- and third-century publications that state that Jesus was present at creation.[29] As he continues, Theophilus references the biography of Jesus of Nazareth as it was told in the preceding gospel books: Jesus "came to what was his own, and his own people did not accept him." And he adds that those who accepted Jesus and believed in him are the true "children of God."[30]

Theophilus's preface is followed by three comments from the editors. In their first comment, the editors make sure that readers understand that the term *Word* is used in a poetic way by Theophilus and represents Jesus of Nazareth. They explain, "The Word became flesh and lived among us." The editors, as so often, speak in first-person plural: "We have seen his glory."

In their second remark, and in typical fashion, the editors cross-reference the character John the Baptist with a passage in the manuscript of the Beloved Disciple, where John the Baptist testified, "He who comes after me ranks ahead of me because he was before me."[31]

The third comment follows the pattern of general statements that are sometimes included in the editorial notes. The terms "fullness," "grace," and the "Law of Moses" are such general topics. Using first-person plural, "We have all received" distinguishes the voice of the editors from the voice of Theophilus and from the voice of John.

After this introductory meditation by Theophilus and three footnotes by the editors, the title of the manuscript of the Beloved Disciple is quoted, "'The Testimony of John.'"[32] The perspective shifts from publisher and editor to the eyewitness perspective of the Beloved Disciple John.[33]

• • •

The implied publisher, Theophilus, is presenting to readers of his Four-Gospel volume, a previously unpublished manuscript written by the Beloved Disciple John, which he had editors carefully prepare for publication.

The editors do not hide their voices. Their comments sometimes cross-reference passages in the manuscript; sometimes they provide background information from outside the text; sometimes they are written in first-person plural, stating their opinions, and sometimes they add lengthy general statements that interrupt the narrative flow. By carefully indicating their own voice and distinguishing it from the voice of the Beloved Disciple, the editors show respect and appreciation for the manuscript. The eyewitness account of the Beloved Disciple and the editorial remarks often clarify, expand, or correct something that had been stated in one or more of the preceding three gospel books. Mixed in with narrative passages, John's manuscript presents a series of monologues of Jesus. Hints in the text suggest that in these speeches John recorded what the Spirit revealed to him after Jesus's death and resurrection.

Revelation of John

The reading strategy to distinguish between the voices of the publisher, editors, author, and the voice of the Spirit works for Revelation of John as well.[34]

Publisher, Author, Spirit, Editors

At the beginning of the book, the implied publisher, Theophilus, states that his editorial goal was to bring John's manuscript about "the revelation of Jesus Christ, which God gave him (John) to show his servants what must soon take place" into a form that a person "who reads aloud the words" could perform before an audience.[35] As with Gospel according to John, the publisher asserts the existence of an autograph, a manuscript written by John with his own hand.[36]

Whereas the implied publisher, Theophilus, talks about the implied author, John, in the third person, John writes his manuscript in the first-person singular, "I, John, . . . was on the island called Patmos because of the word of God and the testimony of Jesus." John explains that he heard a voice that commanded him to "write in a book" what he saw, and it is this manuscript that the publisher had editors prepare for publication.[37]

The episodes of the narrative almost always begin with a passage written by John in the first person and segue into general descriptions with no mention of John. Whereas the passages written in the first person formally fit the description of an eyewitness report, the following sections report events from an omniscient and omnipresent perspective. These passages are like the monologues of Jesus in Gospel according to John, which capture the voice of the Spirit. Using the expression of the publisher of Revelation of John, these passages "show his servants what must soon take place."[38]

Editorial comments were sometimes added to John's manuscript the same way they were added to Gospel according to John, interrupting the voice of "the Spirit." For example, the Spirit says, "I will give permission . . ." and the editors interrupt the speech and talk about the Spirit in the third person: "listen to what the Spirit is saying to the churches!"[39] Also, this comment displays an editorial perspective because it references a section of John's manuscript and not just one sentence, the section where John wrote down "what the Spirit is saying to the churches," something an editor can articulate better than a live character who does not know how the plot will develop.

The implied publisher, in his note to the readers, said that the final form of Revelation of John was produced to be read aloud in front of an audience. Therefore, editorial remarks should not interrupt the flow of speech or digress the way footnotes often do. Instead, they may repeat the central message, address the audience directly, or apply a prophecy to a present conflict, like a "choir" would in a theater production from antiquity.

When John conveys his vision of "a beast rising out of the sea," for example, the editorial comment abandons the narrative setting, in which John is listening to the divine messenger.[40] Addressing readers directly, the editors apply the passage from John's manuscript to the audience's situation, who seem to feel persecuted by their government, and suggest that readers endure being arrested and not start an armed rebellion: "If you are to be taken captive, into captivity you go! If you kill with the sword, with the sword you must be killed!"[41]

Many episodes begin with the perspective of John, followed by the voice of the Spirit, and conclude with an editorial note that makes the vision relevant to the readers. A possible dramatization of the script could assign the passages in the first-person singular to one actor representing John, have another person present the voice of the Spirit, and have a liturgical leader or a choir recite the editorial remark, which professes the moral of the story or gives liturgical instructions.[42]

End of the Book

At the end of his manuscript, John writes, "I, John, am the one who heard and saw these things."[43] Then the narrative switches to Jesus's voice: "Do not seal up the words of the prophecy of this book!" interrupted by an editorial aside: "Blessed are those who wash their robes, so that they will have the right to the tree of life and may enter the city by the gates," and followed by liturgical instructions: "Let the Spirit and the bride . . . and everyone who hears say, 'Come.'"

The liturgical instruction leads back to the beginning of the book, in which the implied publisher, Theophilus, referenced the angel and John and stated that he wanted the book to be read to an audience.[44] The shift between the first-person singular, which here represents the voice of the resurrected Christ, and the voice of the editors speaking about "the Spirit and the bride" is apparent.[45]

Then the voice switches to the first person, and the publisher addresses the readers directly.

> I warn *everyone who hears the words of the prophecy of* this book: *if anyone adds to them, God will add to that person the plagues described in* this book; *if anyone takes away from the words of the* book of this prophecy, *God will take away that person's share in the tree of life and in the holy city, which are described in* this book. (*Rev 22:18–19*)

The shift to first-person singular, "I warn," with its clear reference to "this book," has a direct parallel in the last sentences of Gospel according to John: "But there are also many other things that Jesus did; if every one of them were written down, *I suppose* that the world itself could not contain *the books* that would be written" (John 21:25). In both writings, this is the voice of the implied publisher, Theophilus, the person who authorized the publication of the manuscripts of the Beloved Disciple. Theophilus is protecting his copyright.[46]

The book ends with a promise from the Spirit of Jesus to return soon.[47] The congregants reply, "Come, Lord Jesus!" and the editors conclude the book like most letters of Paul close, with a wish of grace, "The grace of the Lord Jesus be with all the saints. Amen."[48]

• • •

Theophilus, the implied publisher of Revelation of John, presented the book in a similar way as he did with Gospel according to John. He published the first edition of an autograph written by John, Beloved Disciple of Jesus. Both manuscripts consisted of an eyewitness account and a transcript of the words of the Spirit that John received. Both books begin with the publisher's introduction to John's manuscript and contain a personal remark from the publisher at the end, written in the first-person singular.

The genre of both books, however, is different. Whereas Gospel according to John was presented as an annotated edition of an eyewitness report, Revelation of John presents John's manuscript as a script for dramatic public performance.

Letters of John

Theophilus presents three more writings by John. They are numbered, and he entitled them 1, 2, and 3 John.[49] As they are part of the letter collection of the Praxapostolos volume, ancient and modern publishers of the Christian Bible like to add the genre designation "letter" to the title. On closer inspection, however, this classification is only accurate for two of them. The third one is based on an autograph written "with pen and ink."[50] It is addressed to Gaius and serves as a cover note for the second writing, to which John refers in 3 John with, "I have writ-ten something to the church."[51] But what about 1 John?

First John

First John is not a letter. The typical formal elements of a letter are missing. The opening sentences name neither the letter writer nor the addressee, nor do they offer a greeting. Several times, however, the author, John, addresses the readers directly and uses the first-person singular, "I am writing this to you," an expression typical for letters, or more specifically, for autographs. As Theophilus presented Gospel according to John and Revelation of John as a faithful edition of autographs, the same reading instructions apply: First Letter of John is an edition of a text written in the hand of John.[52] And like with the other writings, readers are expected to distinguish between the voices of the author, editors, and publisher.

Prologue

Theophilus presented the introductory passages of Gospel according to John and Revelation of John in his own voice. Why not expect the voice of the publisher in the opening of First Letter of John as well? The parallels between the opening of 1 John and the prologue of Gospel according to John are striking.

1 John 1:1–5	John 1:1.3–5, 12–13
We declare to you what was ❶*from the beginning*, what we have heard, what we have seen with our eyes, what we have looked at and touched with our hands, concerning the ❷*word* of ❸*life*—this life was revealed, and we have seen it and testify to it, and declare to you	❶*In the beginning* was the ❷*Word*, and the Word was with God, and the Word was God. He was in the beginning with God. All things came into being through him, and without him not one thing came into being. What has come into being in him was ❸*life*, and the life was

the eternal life that was with the Father and was revealed to us— we declare to you what we have seen and heard so that you also may have fellowship with us; and truly our ❹ *fellowship is with the Father and with his Son Jesus Christ.* ❺ *We are writing these things* so that our joy may be complete. This is the ❻ *message* we *have heard from him* and proclaim to you, that ❼ *God is light and in him there is no darkness* at all.	the ❼ *light of all people. The light shines in the darkness, and the darkness did not overcome it.* . . . But to all who received him, who believed in his name, he gave power to become ❹ *children of God*, who were born, not of blood or of the will of the flesh or of the will of man, but of God. John 21:24 This is the disciple who is testifying to the things and ❺ *has written them*, and we know that ❻ *his testimony* is true.

Theophilus knows that the readers of the Canonical Edition have access to both texts and use cross-references. That the Word has become flesh in Jesus of Nazareth is more than "what we have heard" and includes "what we have seen with our eyes, what we have looked at and touched with our hands." And what 1 John calls "the word of life" reminds readers of the publisher's reference to the creation narrative of Genesis in his prologue to John's gospel book: Through God's word, "life" was created.

Theophilus declares to readers of the Canonical Edition: "This is the message that we have heard from him (John) and proclaim to you."[53] And he insinuates that "we"—the editors and the publisher— had quite literally "looked at and touched with our own hands" the autographs of John.[54]

This prologue to 1 John applies to all five autographs of John, which Theophilus presents to the public in his New Testament for the first time.

Annotated Autograph

Following the prologue, Theophilus provides a transcript of John's autograph with six editorial comments.[55]

> *My little children, I am writing these things to you so that*
> *you may not* sin.

*1 But if anyone does *sin,* we have an advocate with the Father, Jesus Christ the righteous; and he is the atoning sacrifice for our sins, and not for ours only but also for the sins of the whole world. Now by this we may be sure that we know him, if we obey his commandments. Whoever says, "I have come to know him," but does not obey his commandments, is a liar, and in such a person the truth does not exist; but whoever obeys his word, truly in this person the love of God has reached perfection. By this we may be sure that we are in him: whoever says, "I abide in him," ought to walk just as he walked.

> *Beloved, I am writing you no new commandment, but*
> *an* old commandment *that you have had from the*
> *beginning.*

*2 The *old commandment* is the word that you have heard.

> *Yet I am writing you a new commandment that is true in*
> *him and in you, because the darkness is passing away and the*
> *true* light *is already shining.*

*3 Whoever says, "I am in the *light*," while hating a brother or sister, is still in the darkness. Whoever loves a brother or sister lives in the light, and in such a person there is no cause for stumbling. But whoever hates another believer is in the darkness, walks in the darkness, and does not know the way to go, because the darkness has brought on blindness.

I am writing to you, little children, because your sins are
forgiven on account of his name. I am writing to you, fathers,
because you know him who is from the beginning. I am writing
to you, young people, because you have conquered the evil one. I
write to you, children, because you know the Father. I write to
you, fathers, because you know him who is from the beginning. I
write to you, young people, because you are strong and the word
of God abides in you, and you have overcome the evil one.

*4 Do not love *the world* or the things in the world. The love of
the Father is not in those who love the world; for all that is
in the world—the desire of the flesh, the desire of the eyes,
the pride in riches—comes not from the Father but from
the world. And the world and its desire are passing away, but
those who do the will of God live forever. Children, it is the
last hour! As you have heard that *antichrist* is coming, so now
many antichrists have come. From this we know that it is the
last hour. They went out from us, but they did not belong to
us; for if they had belonged to us, they would have remained
with us. But by going out they made it plain that none of
them belongs to us. But you have been anointed by the Holy
One, and all of you have knowledge.

I write to you, not because you do not know the truth, but
because you know it, and you know that no lie *comes from*
the truth.

*5 Who is the *liar* but the one who denies that Jesus is the Christ?
This is the antichrist, the one who denies the Father and the
Son. No one who denies the Son has the Father; everyone
who confesses the Son has the Father also. Let what you
heard from the beginning abide in you. If what you heard
from the beginning abides in you, then you will abide in the
Son and in the Father. And this is what he has promised us,
eternal life.

> *I write these things to you concerning* those who would
> deceive you.

> *6 As for you, the anointing that you received from him abides in
> you, and so you do not need anyone to teach you. But as his
> anointing teaches you about all things, and *is true and is not a
> lie*, and just as it has taught you, abide in him.

The editorial commentary links to expressions in John's autograph like
it does in Gospel according to John.[56] In their first note, the editors
reference the word "sin" in John's text and switch from the singular to
first-person plural: "We have an advocate with the Father, Jesus Christ
the righteous." The remark is general and timeless. The second annotation references the expression "old commandment" in John's text. The
third one comments on the word "light." The fourth note references
"the evil one" by connecting him to "the love of the world" and calling him the "antichrist."[57] The fifth note connects through the word
"lie" and interprets it as another reference to antichrists. The sixth note
reacts to the expression "those who would deceive you" with the asser-
tion that "the anointing that you received" is "true and is not a lie" and
that the anointing confirms John's message independently.

Homily

Following the annotated autograph, Theophilus presents a homily,
speaking again in first-person plural. At the center stand two statements: that Jesus was human and not a ghost, and that God is invisible
and can be experienced in the community of believers through love.[58]
In the end, he returns to the beginning of his homily and declares that
only those who stay in Christ will receive life.[59]

Epilogue

The epilogue, which has parallels in Gospel according to John and
Revelation of John, is introduced through a final quote from John's
autograph, followed up with an editorial annotation.[60]

I write these things to you who believe in the name of the Son of God, so that you may know that you have eternal life.

*7 And this is the boldness we have in him, that if *we ask anything according to his will*, he hears us. And if we know that he hears us in whatever we ask, we know that we have obtained the requests made of him.

And then Theophilus briefly slips into first-person singular, as he had done at the end of Gospel according to John and Revelation of John: "There is sin that is mortal; *I do not say* that you should pray about that."[61]

In conclusion, Theophilus sums up the Christological narrative featured in the Canonical Edition: "And we know that the *Son of God* has come and has given us understanding so *that we may know* him who is true; and we are in him who is true, in his Son Jesus Christ. He is the true God and *eternal life*. Little children, *keep yourselves from idols*."[62] God has sent his Son Jesus Christ into the world to offer redemption from death through knowledge of the truth. All other concepts are lies.

Structure and Literary Genre

Theophilus, who oversees the edition of Gospel according to John and Revelation of John, publishes another autograph of John in 1 John. He introduces it, as was his habit, with a prologue, annotates the autograph, and adds a homily and an epilogue as he prepares the text for publication.

By quoting the autograph and placing it at the center of the publication, Theophilus wants to convince readers of its authenticity. In the autographic portion of 1 John, John addresses children, fathers, and young men. They need confirmation and appreciation of what they know and do more than they need instruction. John speaks about why he is writing and whom he is writing for, but he does not say which writings he is referring to. The editorial narrative of the Canonical Edition gives an answer: John is talking about the autographs published in Gospel according to John, Revelation of John, and what

Theophilus entitled 2 and 3 John. And therefore, the genre of 1 John is a cover note by the publisher, introducing his edition of five autographic manuscripts of the Beloved Disciple John.[63]

Second John

Second John is a letter written to a congregation, and 3 John addresses a single person, Gaius. By placing the two letters side by side, Theophilus suggests that 2 John is the writing that John references in 3 John when he says, "I wrote something to the church."[64] The editorial narrative offers both John's official message to the community in 2 John and John's personal agenda, which he shares with a trusted friend in 3 John. Theophilus added only one editorial comment.[65]

The ending of Second Letter of John suggests that the letter is an autograph: "Although I have much to write to you, I would rather not use paper and ink; instead, I hope to come to you and talk with you face to face, so that our joy may be complete."[66]

Third John

Third John is also a letter and only slightly longer than 2 John. Its confidential nature indicates that John wrote the short note without the help of a secretary but in his own hand and that the letter was not meant to be read to the congregation. The negative remarks about Diotrephes would certainly not have gone over well with Diotrephes sitting in the audience.[67]

> *I have written something to the church; but* Diotrephes, *who likes to put himself first, does not acknowledge our authority. So, if I come, I will call attention to what he is doing in spreading false charges against us.*

For lack of an alternative location, Patmos becomes the place where John stayed as he wrote the letters that Theophilus incorporated into the Canonical Edition as 2 and 3 John.[68]

Gaius in the Editorial Narrative

Gaius is a significant character in Theophilus's editorial narrative. He is the host of Paul in Corinth when Paul writes his Letter to Romans, and he is mentioned in 1 Corinthians as one of the few who were baptized by Paul.[69] Gaius is close to Paul and John, like Mark and Luke are close to Paul and Peter. They all serve as role models because they demonstrate the unity of the Catholic Christian Church. But Gaius is also associated with Ephesus. From Acts, readers learn that he was originally from Derbe in Lycaonia and that he and Paul were dragged into the theater in Ephesus by the mob.[70]

That Theophilus could produce a document of such a private nature provides credibility to Theophilus's claim of having had access to autographs. It also gives Gaius an important role in the implied provenance narrative. Mark and Luke contribute books to Theophilus's Canonical Edition, and Gaius delivers at least one if not all of John's autographs.

• • •

Theophilus's editorial narrative of the Canonical Edition assigned five unpublished manuscripts to John, the Beloved Disciple of Jesus. He incorporated John's gospel manuscript as Gospel according to John into the Four-Gospel volume of the Canonical Edition. The prophetic manuscript he gave the title Revelation of John. Theophilus numbered the three short autographs for editorial consistency and included them in the letter section of the Praxapostolos, carefully indicating what were quotes from John's manuscripts and what was editorial commentary. First John serves as a cover note, authenticating all of John's manuscripts; 2 and 3 John prove to the sympathetic reader that Theophilus also had access to autographs of John of a rather private nature.

This is as far as a literary approach can carry the reader. And this is the point where a historical approach must take the lead.

VI

THE ORIGIN OF THE CANONICAL EDITION

IT IS IMPORTANT to distinguish between document and literature, and between story and history, to appreciate the difference between historical and implied authors, editors, and publishers. It is this difference that makes it possible to recognize the design of the Canonical Edition of the New Testament and to speculate about who was involved in its first publication.

Historical publishers of edited collections usually speak with the voice of the implied publisher to promote their own views. Theophilus, naturally, cannot reference the Marcionite Edition, as it did not yet exist during the lifetime of Paul, the setting of the Canonical Edition's editorial narrative. The historical publisher wanted to replace the Marcionite Edition with his own revised and enlarged version.

Therefore, in addition to Theophilus's commentary on John's writings, the interpolations to the Marcionite Edition and the editorial setting of the added writings, may also provide clues to identify the second-century historical publisher of the Canonical Edition.

§10
Interpolations

The first documented readers of the Canonical Edition, Justin, Clement of Alexandria, Irenaeus, and Tertullian, agree on three differences between the Canonical Edition and the Marcionite Edition. First, the Canonical Edition demonstrates that the promises of God in the prophetic writings of Israel were fulfilled in Jesus, whereas the Marcionite

Edition did not elaborate on Jesus as the fulfillment of prophetic predictions. Second, in the Canonical Edition, the Creator is the Father of Jesus, whereas the Marcionite Edition promoted the concept of a Demiurge. And third, in the editorial narrative of the Canonical Edition, Paul eventually settles his disagreements with Jesus's disciples and brothers, but in the Marcionite Edition, that conflict was never resolved. All three topics are reflected in identifiable interpolations to the Marcionite Edition.

When the historical publisher spoke as Theophilus, he wanted readers to distinguish between the voice of John and editorial additions. In the writings attributed to Luke and Paul, however, he did not want his additions to be recognized. The comparison of Gospel according to Luke with the older Marcionite Edition reveals an abundance of unmarked interpolations, which add about 50 percent of text.[1]

Gospel According to Luke

In the Four-Gospel volume, the name "Luke" is only mentioned in the title and not in the text of the third gospel book.[2] He shares this fate with Mark and John, who are also not mentioned in the text of their gospel books. According to the editorial narrative, Luke finishes Acts of Apostles while Paul is in Rome. Paul corroborates that "Luke is with me" in Second Letter to Timothy, which Paul writes from Rome, expecting to die soon.[3]

In Letter to Colossians, Paul portrays Luke as a physician.[4] Luke is personally acquainted with Mark, the author of one of his sources; he knows Onesimus, who is the fugitive slave mentioned in Paul's letter to Philemon; and he met Gaius, who hosts Paul in Corinth, three important characters of the editorial narrative.[5] And according to Luke's own report in Acts of Apostles, he joins Paul on his trip from Corinth via Macedonia and Miletus to Jerusalem and from there to Rome.[6]

Therefore, from Theophilus's perspective, Luke had intimate and personal knowledge of Paul during the last year of his ministry in Asia Minor and Greece, his arrest in Jerusalem, and his transfer to Rome as a prisoner. Luke certainly would have had access to Paul's letters and his library, which he asked Timothy to bring from Troas to Rome.[7] As a physician, Luke was well educated and was able to research and write.

In his prologue to the first volume, the gospel book, Luke laid out his writing project.[8] He had studied books about Jesus written by other authors, he had organized the information, interviewed witnesses, and now submitted his work to Theophilus for publication.[9] His purpose was to critically review the tradition.[10]

Luke's First-century Narrative	Publisher's Second-century Message
Since many have undertaken to set down an orderly account of the events that have been fulfilled among us,	• *Many publications about Jesus and his first followers exist and compete with the Canonical Edition.*
just as they were handed on to us by those who from the beginning were eyewitnesses and servants of the word,	• *The Canonical Edition is based on eyewitness accounts (Matthew, James, John, Peter, Jude) and the writings of servants of the word (Mark and Paul).*
I too decided,	• *Luke is a first-century author*
after investigating everything carefully from the very first, to write an orderly account	• *who carefully researched the evidence and reconstructed the sequence of events,*
for you, most excellent Theophilus,	• *and who submitted his manuscript for publication to Theophilus,*
so that you may know the truth concerning the things about which you have been instructed.	• *To let the public know what really happened.*

The identification of this passage as an addition to the Marcionite Gospel, however, indicates that the historical publisher uses the voice of

Luke as a literary device, the same way he uses the voice of Theophilus for the Johannine writings. Like Theophilus, literary Luke is created by the historical publisher's imagination.

God's Promises through the Prophets Are Fulfilled in Jesus

And what message does the historical publisher want to pass on?

Two examples, one from the first sentences and one from the last sentences of the Marcionite Gospel, demonstrate that many of these interpolations promote the concept that Jesus is the fulfillment of Jewish prophecies.[11]

The first sentence of the Marcionite gospel book gives the fifteenth year of Tiberius as the date and has an unknown character walk down to "Capharnaum, a city in Galilee," where people call him "Jesus of Nazareth."[12] Jesus drives out an unclean spirit, returns to his hometown Nazareth, and enters the synagogue to worship. At this point, the editors of Gospel according to Luke interpolate the text.[13]

> But when he came to Nazara, he went into the synagogue on the Sabbath day {+ **as was his custom. He stood up to read, and the scroll of the prophet Isaiah was given to him. He unrolled the scroll and found the place where it was written: "The Spirit of the Lord is upon me, because he has anointed me to bring good news to the poor. He has sent me to proclaim release to the captives and recovery of sight to the blind, to let the oppressed go free, to proclaim the year of the Lord's favor." And he rolled up the scroll, gave it back to the attendant, and sat down. The eyes of all in the synagogue were fixed on him. Then he began to say to them, "Today this scripture has been fulfilled in your hearing." All spoke well of him and were amazed at the gracious words that came from his mouth** +}. And they said, "Is not this Joseph's son?" And he said to them, "Now you will indubitably quote this proverb to me, 'Physician, heal yourself! Everything that we have heard happening

in Capharnaum, do also here in your hometown.'" But he said, "Truly, I say to you: No prophet is accepted in his hometown. {+ **But the truth is, there were many widows in Israel in the time of Elijah, when the heaven was shut up three years and six months, and there was a severe famine over all the land; yet Elijah was sent to none of them except to a widow at Zarephath in Sidon. There were also many lepers in Israel in the time of the prophet Elisha, and none of them was cleansed except Naaman the Syrian. +}**" Then all in the synagogue were filled with anger, and they got up and thrust him out of the city. And they led him to the slope of the mountain on which their city is built to hurl him down. But he passed right through the midst of them and went away.

The first interpolation has Jesus read to the congregation from the Isaiah scroll and declare that the prophecies are now fulfilled. He sits down, and all are amazed "at the gracious words that came from his mouth." Only a few sentences later, when Jesus refers to the saying that "no prophet is accepted in his hometown," the editors add another lengthy interpolation. They tell the Biblical story of Elijah and the widow of Zarephath in Sidon, giving scriptural validation of the unbiblical proverb and apologetically defending that Jesus did not heal in Nazareth: "There were also many lepers in Israel in the time of the prophet Elisha."[14]

At the end of the Marcionite Gospel, three days after the crucifixion, the resurrected Jesus appears to two disciples who are leaving Jerusalem. He tells them, "You are without understanding." The editors turn the affirmative "For it was necessary that Christ suffers all this" into a question, "Was it necessary?" They add, "Then beginning with Moses and all the prophets, he interpreted to them the things about himself in all the scriptures."[15]

And when Jesus appears to the twelve and eats "a piece of roasted fish," an editorial interpolation repeats the same statement: "Everything written about me in the law of Moses, the prophets, and the psalms must be fulfilled."[16]

> But when they were still disbelieving, he said to them, "Have you something here to eat?" And they gave him a piece of roasted fish. And he took it and ate it before their eyes. {- ~~And the rest he gave to them.~~ -} {+ **Then he said to them, "These are my words that I spoke to you while I was still with you—that everything written about me in the law of Moses, the prophets, and the psalms must be fulfilled." Then he opened their minds to understand the scriptures, and he said to them, "Thus it is written, that the Messiah is to suffer and to rise from the dead on the third day, and that repentance and forgiveness of sins is to be proclaimed in his name to all nations, beginning from Jerusalem. You are witnesses of these things. And see, I am sending upon you what my Father promised; so, stay here in the city until you have been clothed with power from on high"** +}.

In each of these interpolations, the editors use the voice of Jesus as they open the readers' minds to understand "the scriptures."[17] And they demonstrate how the scriptural prophets of Israel had projected Jesus's ministry and message.[18]

Ten Letters of Paul

Opening and Conclusion
Gospel according to John, 1 John, and Revelation of John show that the historical publisher favors the opening and conclusion of a book for editorial comments when he speaks with the voice of Theophilus. The beginning of Gospel according to Luke and the end of Letter to Romans also contain elaborate unmarked interpolations. Therefore, the introduction to the Fourteen-Letters-of-Paul volume and its conclusion are typical places for the historical publisher to consider interpolations to the traditional text.

In the very first sentence of Letter to Romans, Paul endorses "the gospel of God" and the "prophets in the holy scriptures," which to a later audience reads like an endorsement of the Four-Gospel volume and the authority of Jewish Scriptures.[19] More specifically, literary Paul defines the content of the "gospel of God" as a proclamation that Jesus was related to "David according to the flesh" and that "according to the spirit" Jesus was "Son of God," which is demonstrated in his "resurrection from the dead."[20]

The Marcionite Gospel lacks an explanation of where Jesus came from at the beginning and where he went at the end of the book, which does not satisfy Paul's definition of the "gospel of God." Mark's gospel book also lacked an explanation of how Jesus of Nazareth could possibly be related to the house of David, and it offered not a single appearance of the resurrected Christ. Gospel according to Luke, however, perfectly fulfills the requirements of Paul's definition: Luke presented Jesus as the fulfillment of prophetic promises; he explained how Jesus was related to King David; he reported two appearances of the resurrected Christ in Jerusalem before the gospel book concluded.[21] Paul's definition of his apostleship as "to bring about the obedience of faith among all the nations" reflects Luke's storyline in his book about the apostles, which follows Paul from Antioch in Syria through Asia Minor to Europe.[22]

The connections between the beginning of Letter to Romans to the Four-Gospel volume, the link to the storyline of Acts of Apostles, and the canonical editors' concept of promoting Jewish Scriptures as promises that are fulfilled in Jesus, so clearly represent the canonical editors' agenda that one must suspect a rather heavy-handed interpolation to the Marcionite Edition. It would explain the convoluted sentence structure of the untypically long opening. Unfortunately, the wording of this passage in the Marcionite Edition is not attested.[23]

The Fourteen-Letters-of-Paul volume concludes with the Letter to Philemon. In this letter, Paul asks Philemon to take back a slave, Onesimus, who had run away. Paul writes a legally binding promissory note with his own hand that he "will repay" Philemon all damages that the loss of his slave may have caused.[24] Again, Theophilus signals that he had access to the autograph. And even for the most casual readers, the characters mentioned at the end of the letter link the Fourteen-Letters-of-Paul volume to Theophilus's editorial narrative.

> Epaphras, *my fellow prisoner in Christ Jesus, sends greetings to you, and so do* Mark, Aristarchus, Demas, *and* Luke, *my fellow workers. (Philemon 23–25)*

"Mark" and "Luke," the authors of two gospel books, and "Epaphras" who visited Paul in prison and carried Letter to Colossians back, send their greetings. All three are with Paul in Rome. Demas is mentioned in Second Letter to Timothy, which is missing in the Marcionite Edition, and Aristarchus is a character in Acts of Apostles and connects the Praxapostolos with the Fourteen-Letters-of-Paul volume.[25]

The editorial passages at the beginning of 1 John, Gospel according to John, Revelation of John, Gospel according to Matthew, Gospel according to Mark, and at the end of Letter to Romans either explicitly reference Jewish scriptures or mention characters that connect the writings and volumes of the Canonical Edition. This observation makes it probable that the beginning and the end of the Fourteen-Letters-of-Paul volume were interpolated.[26]

Traditionally, interpreters of these passages simply assumed that Paul had written them. This confidence is not warranted. If the passage supports the editorial narrative of the Canonical Edition, it could just as well be an addition to the text of the Marcionite Edition, which is the only witness to the letters of Paul. We cannot know for sure whether these texts are quotes from the Marcionite Edition, or a canonical addition.

Paul Made Peace with James

In antiquity, a shorter version of Paul's letter to Rome is attested. The last part, which in modern printed editions are chapters 15 and 16, was missing.[27] Origen insisted that this shorter form was the text of the Marcionite Edition.[28] Consequently, the last two chapters of Letter to Romans constitute an interpolation by the editors of the Canonical Edition. The wish for peace and an explicit "Amen" at the end of chapter 15 mark the end of the part that the scribe wrote.[29] The postscript that follows was written in Paul's hand, another one of Theophilus's astonishing autographs.

In First Letter to Corinthians, Paul worries about whether the Macedonians and Corinthians can raise enough money to make an unplanned trip to Jerusalem worth his while.[30] The Marcionite Edition never makes mention of Paul traveling from Corinth to Jerusalem but includes several letters written from Rome and leaves it up to the readers to fill in the gap. The rather obvious suggestion is that Paul traveled directly from Corinth to Rome, which in return implies that his fundraising campaign in Macedonia and Achaia had not been successful.[31]

The canonical interpolation, however, fills in the blanks differently. It reports that Paul's fundraising campaign in Macedonia and Corinth was a success and that Paul made the trip to Jerusalem before continuing to Rome.

> *At present, however, I am going to Jerusalem in a ministry to the saints; for Macedonia and Achaia have been pleased to share their resources with the poor among the saints at Jerusalem. (Rom 15:25–26)*

Whereas according to the Marcionite Edition, Paul writes the letter in preparation for his upcoming trip to Rome, in the Canonical Edition, he writes to postpone it and instead leaves for Jerusalem.[32] Acts of Apostles supports the storyline of the interpolation.[33] Taking cues from the passion story of Jesus, the narrative of Acts has Paul entering Jerusalem, "unbelievers" opposing Paul, and Roman authorities arresting him. Jesus's brother James welcomes Paul, but in the end, he and "all the elders" are powerless.[34] Paul is arrested and sent to Rome for a trial.

In the interpolated postscript, Paul recommends Phoebe. Paul passes the pen to Tertius, who writes a sentence, "I Tertius, the writer of this letter, greet you in the Lord." Tertius returns the pen to Paul, who finishes with personal greetings.

> *Timothy, my co-worker, greets you; so do Lucius . . . I Tertius, the writer of this letter, greet you in the Lord. Gaius, who is host to me and to the whole church, greets you. Erastus, the city treasurer, and our brother Quartus, greet you. (Romans 16:21–23)*

In his handwritten greetings, Paul mentions Luke, Timothy, and Gaius, three characters who feature prominently in the editorial narrative of the Canonical Edition. Timothy is the recipient of two letters that the editors added to the Marcionite Edition of Paul. And Lucius, the Latinized form of "Luke," is the author of Gospel according to Luke and Acts of Apostles. The character Gaius provides a cross-link between the Letter to Romans, Acts of Apostles, First Letter to Corinthians, and Third Letter of John.[35]

With this seemingly trivial sentence, the interpolators not only endorse the author of Acts and his "passion story" of Paul, but they also connect the Fourteen-Letters-of-Paul volume with the Four-Gospel volume and the Praxapostolos.[36]

Moving back to the perspective of Theophilus: By publishing the text of the autograph, Theophilus implies that he has seen the writing sample and can attest that Tertius was the scribe who had made the copy of Romans which he is now editing for publication and which included two chapters missing in the Marcionite Edition.[37] The historical publisher is using the character of Theophilus to authenticate the interpolation and make the Marcionite Edition look defective.[38]

The most important outcome of adding two chapters at the end of Letter to Romans, however, is the endorsement of Luke's report that James assisted Paul during his fateful visit to Jerusalem. James and Paul were friends, not enemies.

Denial of the Demiurge

According to Irenaeus, Clement of Alexandria, and Tertullian, Catholic Christians debated with competing Christian groups whether the world was created by the God of Jesus or by a lesser divinity, the Demiurge. Tertullian attests a passage in Paul's Letter to Colossians that was missing in the Marcionite Edition.[39] The editors add an interpolation after the expression "the image of the invisible God."

> (The Father) has rescued us from the power of darkness and transferred us into the kingdom of his beloved Son, in whom we have redemption, the forgiveness of sins. He is the image of the invisible God {+, **the firstborn of all creation; for in him all things in heaven and on earth were created, things visible and invisible, whether thrones or dominions or rulers or powers—all things have been created through him and for him. He himself is before all things, and in him all things hold together +**}. He is the head of the body, the church; he is the beginning, the firstborn from the dead, so that he might come to have first place in everything. (Colossians 1:13–18)

Referencing the creation story in Genesis and the editorial prologues of Gospel according to John and First John, the interpolators articulate the position that Jesus is the beloved Son of the god who created the world. They leave no room for the concept of a Demiurge.

• • •

Three of the characteristics of the Canonical Edition that distinguish it from the Marcionite Edition according to early documented readers are featured prominently in interpolations: the New Testament as the fulfillment of Jewish scripture, the denial of the concept of a Demiurge, and the attempt to harmonize the conflict between Paul on one side and Jesus's brothers and disciples on the other side. The peaceful resolution of their conflict provides the canvas on which the historical publisher paints his political vision of a Catholic Christian Church.

§11
Additional Writings

Gospels According to Matthew and Mark

Matthew's Opening and Conclusion
When Theophilus mentions that Luke studied eyewitness reports, he immediately created a link to the eyewitness account of Matthew.

The first time Matthew is mentioned in Gospel according to Matthew, he is introduced as an eyewitness, a tax collector.[40] Later, Jesus calls "Matthew the tax collector" to become one of the twelve disciples.[41] When Jesus explains the message of the parables to his disciples in a private meeting, Matthew receives privileged information about "the secrets of the kingdom of heaven."[42]

And at the end of the gospel book, when the resurrected Christ appears to the eleven faithful disciples, Matthew is present.

> *Now the eleven disciples went to Galilee, to the mountain*
> *to which Jesus had directed them. When they saw him, they*
> *worshiped him; but some doubted. And Jesus came and said*
> *to them, "All authority in heaven and on earth has been given*
> *to me. Go therefore and make disciples of all nations. "*
> *(Matthew 28:16–19)*

Obedient to Jesus Christ's final command, to go out and make disciples of "all nations," Matthew writes this book in Greek, the language of "all nations."

Although Theophilus added the title "Gospel according to Matthew" for consistency within the Four-Gospel volume, he preserved Matthew's title: "Book, [of] Genesis, [of] Jesus, Christ."[43]

There are several valid ways to translate the four words into English. The NRSV translation, "an account of the genealogy of Jesus the Messiah," is informed by the list of Jesus's ancestors that follows.

Alternatively, the first two words, Book of Genesis, playfully recall the title of the first book of the Old Testament. For the Canonical Edition's effort to promote the "New Testament" as the fulfillment of Jewish scriptures, Matthew's title is meaningful on this very literal level.[44]

But the word *genesis* can also be linked to the following "Jesus Christ," allowing readers to understand the title as "A book about how Jesus became Christ," which would capture Matthew's storyline that begins with Jesus's human ancestry and ends with the appearance of the divine Christ on the mountain in Galilee.

As so often in literature and art, even though each interpretation excludes the other two, all three are adequate, appropriate, and true.

The edict of Cyrus at the end of 2 Chronicles forms the final passage in many manuscripts and printed editions of the Hebrew Bible. And just as Matthew's first two words evoke the Book of Genesis, the structure of Christ's final words parallels the end of 2 Chronicles.

Matthew 28:18–20	2 Chronicles 36:23
❶All authority in ❷heaven, and on ❸earth has been ❹given to me. ❺Go therefore and make disciples of all nations, baptizing them in the name of the Father and of the Son and of the Holy Spirit, and teaching them to obey everything that I have ❻commanded you. And remember, ❼I am with you always, to the end of the age.	❶All the kingdoms of the ❸earth has ❹given me the Lord, the God of ❷heaven, and he has ❻charged me to build him a house at Jerusalem, which is in Judah. Whoever is among you of all his people, may the Lord his ❼God be with him! Let him ❺go up.

The implied author, Matthew, begins and ends his work with reference to the beginning and end of the Old Testament's editorial narrative.

Luke's Competing Narrative

Matthew's book and Luke's gospel book share many stories and teachings of Jesus. In his prologue, Luke classified books like Matthew's gospel book as belonging to publications by eyewitnesses. Theophilus did not change the text of Matthew to match the message of Luke. He treated it with the same respect that he had shown when he prepared the manuscript of the Beloved Disciple for publication, leaving it to readers of the Canonical Edition to identify what Luke found useful enough to excerpt from Matthew verbatim and what Luke felt he needed to change.

Luke, for example, did not accept Matthew's version of Jesus's genealogy. He replaced it with another one. Although both genealogies agree that Jesus was related to the house of David, they trace the family back to a different Son of David. Matthew builds the family tree through David's son Solomon and Luke through David's other son Nathan.[45]

Luke also ignored most of Matthew's stories relating to the birth of Jesus. Matthew uses the testimony of Joseph and reports details as personal as his dreams at night. Luke, on the other hand, uses Mary's testimony and reports the very private and intimate story of how the young virgin became pregnant from the angel Gabriel or the story of Mary's visit with Elizabeth when the unborn John the Baptist "leaped inside" Elizabeth, Mary's prayers, Mary giving birth to her son, the story of the shepherds who were sent by angels, Jesus's circumcision, and the traumatic episode when Mary and Joseph were accidentally separated from their twelve-year-old son during a trip to Jerusalem.[46] At the end of Jesus's childhood stories, Luke stated, "His mother kept all these things in her heart."[47] Matthew, however, gives Joseph's version: how Joseph's dreams prohibited him from abandoning pregnant Mary, about the wise men visiting from the East, the escape to Egypt, Herod's massacre of young boys, the family's return from Egypt, and their move to Nazareth. And Matthew is always quick to comment in his own voice that each of the events happened "so that what was spoken by the Lord through the prophet might be fulfilled."[48]

According to Luke's book about Jesus, Jesus ascends to heaven on Easter Sunday evening, leaving no time for Jesus to appear in Galilee as he does in Matthew's account. But in his volume about the apostles, Luke removes the discrepancy. He postpones Jesus's ascension to a Thursday, forty days after Easter Sunday, leaving room for appearances to the disciples in Galilee, which are projected by Mark, reported by Matthew, and confirmed by John.[49]

Few modern readers who read the New Testament within their faith communities notice these differences between Matthew and Luke, although they are very apparent. But the editors of the Canonical Edition almost certainly were aware of them. Competing second- and third-century books on Jesus show the same phenomenon. Although the narratives are presented with the authority of eyewitnesses, narrative discrepancies between reports are not removed. Matthew's gospel book satisfies genre expectations.

Who Is Mark?

Gospel according to Mark, the other gospel book Luke used, also distinguishes between the editorial title, Gospel according to Mark, and Mark's title, "Gospel about Jesus Christ the Son of God."[50]

> *The beginning of the good news* [gospel] *of Jesus Christ, the Son of God. As it is written in the* prophet Isaiah, *"See, I am sending my messenger ahead of you, who will prepare your way; the voice of one crying out in the wilderness: 'Prepare the way of the Lord, make his paths straight.'"* (Mark 1:1–3)

"Prophet Isaiah" references the editorial title of this book in Greek editions of Jewish scriptures, a parallel to Matthew, who mentioned the term *Genesis* in his first sentence.

According to the Fourteen-Letters-of-Paul volume, Luke knew Mark rather well. Twice they are mentioned in the same sentence.[51] In his book on the apostles, Luke, using some discretion concerning embarrassing details, reports that Mark accompanied Paul on his first missionary trip, but Mark failed to live up to Paul's expectations and therefore Paul refused to take Mark on his next trip. Instead, Barnabas, who was Mark's uncle, as Paul explains in his Letter to Colossians, took Mark under his wing.[52] Readers also learn from Paul's Letter to Colossians that Mark and Paul eventually made peace with each other; he recommends Mark to the Colossians.[53] By including First Letter of Peter in the Praxapostolos volume, Theophilus provides the information that Mark was close to Peter, who called him a "son."[54] In the narrative of Acts, Luke calls him John Mark and places him in the social context of Peter.[55]

The implied author, Mark begins his narrative with a brief description of John the Baptist and the baptism of Jesus, followed by the story of Jesus's temptation by Satan. He is setting the stage for the entrance of his main character, Peter, who becomes Jesus's first disciple. From now on, Peter is the central eyewitness to everything that happens. When the women discover the empty tomb at the end of Mark's gospel book, they are told to inform "the disciples and Peter."[56] Peter is highlighted because it is Peter's story that Mark records.[57]

In his first letter, Peter mentioned Mark together with Silvanus, a scribe who had also worked for Paul.[58] And in Second Letter of Peter, Peter expresses a desire to leave a record of what happened.[59] So, Peter told his story, and Mark wrote it down.

To identify Mark, Theophilus expects readers to combine information from the Four-Gospel volume, the Praxapostolos volume, and the Fourteen-Letters-of-Paul volume.

Luke's Criticism of Mark

Luke disliked books on Jesus that were not well organized.[60] And Mark's book certainly belongs to that category; episodes follow each other without necessity.[61]

Luke provides a prequel to Mark's story, describing the birth of Jesus in Bethlehem, and he provides an account of what happened after the women had discovered the empty tomb. In Mark's gospel book, the resurrected Jesus never appears. By adding a prequel and a sequel, Luke, the companion of Paul, fulfills the expectation of Paul, who defines the message of the true gospel in his Letter to Romans: According to the flesh, Jesus is a Son of David, and according to the spirit, Jesus is Son of God, which is demonstrated in Jesus's resurrection.[62] In both aspects, Luke improves on Mark's book.

Arrangement of the Four-Gospel Volume

By placing Luke third in his Four-Gospel volume, Theophilus suggests that Luke used the preceding works of Matthew and Mark.[63] And because the gospel of a disciple was most likely written before a disciple of a disciple wrote his book, Theophilus set Matthew before Mark and used his own discovery, John's gospel book, to conclude the volume. Following this line of interpretation, Theophilus arranged the books in chronological order. His editorial strategy was to rather manipulate the message of the Marcionite Gospel through interpolations and additional writings than through deletions.

Praxapostolos

Acts of Apostles

Another book, and possibly the most important one from the perspective of the historical publisher that was added to the Marcionite Edition to establish the editorial narrative, was Acts of Apostles. Its anti-Marcionite tendency cannot be overlooked. The first part features the disciples and brothers of Jesus, and the second part features Paul. The plural "apostles" in the title indicates that they are all considered to be apostles.

At the beginning of his book, the implied author Luke clarifies that this is the second one in a series and that he picks up the story where it left off, at the ascension of Jesus.[64]

> *In my first book, dear* Theophilus, *I wrote about everything that Jesus* did and taught from the beginning to the day when he was taken up into heaven. *(Acts 1:12)*

As only one of the gospel books of the Canonical Edition is addressed to Theophilus, and because it covers "what Jesus did and taught" and reports events from "the beginning" when Jesus was born to "the day when he was taken up into heaven," Luke undoubtedly refers to his gospel book.[65]

In his second book, Luke indicates by formulating passages in the first-person plural that he was an eyewitness to some but not all reported events. This is a significant difference from his book on Jesus, where he completely relied on the witness of others. The last of these we-passages takes the story to Rome, where Luke concludes his narrative. The story of the book unfolds as the resurrected Christ projected: "You will be my witnesses in Jerusalem [Acts 1–7], in all Judea [Acts 9–12] and Samaria [Acts 8], and to the ends of the earth" [Acts 13–28].[66]

The first half of Acts is dominated by characters who are involved with the early Christian community in Jerusalem, Judea, and Samaria: Jesus's disciples and Jesus's family. They are introduced to readers immediately after the ascension story.[67] In the second half of the book, the main character is the Apostle Paul, who travels "to the ends of the earth." And in the middle of the book, both parties publicly meet for a council in Jerusalem.[68]

As Luke concludes the narrative, he is with Paul in Rome at the end of a two-year stay.[69] Paul is alive and busy when Luke submits the second volume of his manuscript to Theophilus for publication. The implied date is, therefore, the middle of the first century and the implied location is Rome.

Theophilus uses Luke's two books to organize the Canonical Edition. He puts Luke's book on Jesus at the core of the Four-Gospel volume, and he uses Luke's book about the apostles as an introduction to the two letter collections of the Canonical Edition: The Catholic Letters, with letters written by the heroes of the first half of Acts, and the letters of Paul, the hero of the second half of Acts. Whereas the Catholic Letters are appended to Acts of Apostles to form the Praxapostolos, the Fourteen Letters of Paul are published as a separate volume.

In Theophilus's narrative world, Luke must be familiar with the fourteen letters that Paul wrote while they were traveling together. Only these letters are included. This way Luke, the critical historian, becomes a witness to the authenticity of Theophilus's edition of Paul's writings.[70]

By attaching letters of the brothers and disciples of Jesus to Acts of Apostles, Theophilus suggests that Luke also served as the authenticator of the autographs of James, Jude, and Peter. For the authenticity of Letters of John, Theophilus vouches for himself. He arranged the letters in the order that Paul listed the "acknowledged pillars" in Jerusalem, and he added Letter of Jude at the end.[71]

Although Acts does not quote from any letter of Paul or from any of the Catholic epistles, the authors of these letters are the protagonists of Luke's book on the apostles. Because Luke does not cite from the letters, Theophilus can present Luke's narrative the same way he presented Luke's book on Jesus, as a critical assessment of the sources and a careful reconstruction of the events.

Luke concludes the story in Rome while Paul is still alive. Luke was present when Paul and Peter wrote their final letters from Rome: 2 Timothy and 2 Peter. Both authors expect their impending deaths in Rome.[72] In other words, Theophilus purposefully presented Acts of Apostles in the context of the Catholic Letters and the Letters of Paul. Acts explains the letters, and the letters explain Acts.[73]

One of Theophilus's central messages, using the voice of Luke, is that Peter, James, and Paul worked hand in hand, discrediting the editorial narrative of the Marcionite Edition.

Letter of James

In his book on the apostles, Luke mentions James as the leader of "the believers" in Jerusalem.[74] So does Paul in his letters.[75] The information that one of Jesus's brothers is called James is corroborated by the list of Jesus's four brothers given in Gospels according to Matthew and Mark.[76]

Theophilus presents James's letter to document the conflict between James and Paul.[77] Both discuss the relationship between works and faith in their letters, using the same scriptural references but reaching the opposite conclusions.[78]

James 2:23–24	Romans 4:2–3; Galatians 2:16

Thus, the scripture was fulfilled that says, "Abraham believed God, and it was reckoned to him as righteousness," and he was called the friend of God.
 	
    You see that a person is justified by works and not by faith alone.
	For if Abraham was justified by works, he has something to boast about, but not before God. For what does the scripture say? "Abraham believed God, and it was reckoned to him as righteousness."
	
	    We know that a person is justified not by the works of the law but through faith in Jesus Christ.

Luke makes James the first person to speak in support of Paul after the controversial events in Antioch had been laid out before the apostles in Jerusalem. James summarizes the outcome of the meeting, and he coauthors a letter to the diaspora detailing the decisions.[79] His conciliatory spirit makes him the perfect character in Theophilus's editorial narrative to write "Letter of James."[80]

Two Letters of Peter

Like Letter of James, First Letter of Peter is addressed to followers who live in the Dispersion.[81] As there is no distinction made between the recipients of the two letters, the "Second Letter" of Peter is written to the same audience.[82]

    Among the regions addressed in Peter's letters are Galatia and Asia, two regions where Paul was active.[83] Paul's Letter to Galatians is a letter, uncharacteristically written to a region rather than to a city or a person. According to Paul's letter, groups of believers existed in Galatia who were critical of Paul, and Paul mentions his opponents James,

Peter, and John by name, implying that they had followers in Galatia.[84] Ephesus, the capital of the Roman province of Asia, is the recipient of one of Paul's letters. Ephesus is featured prominently in Paul's letters to Corinth, to Timothy, and in Luke's book on the apostles.[85]

So, the editorial narrative informs readers that Peter, following the lead of his colleague James, had also written to believers who lived in a region strongly influenced by Paul.[86]

In the context of Letter of James, Peter's letters also document the background of what had caused the incident between Peter and Paul. First Letter of Peter was written before the clash in Antioch. Second Letter of Peter was written shortly before Peter's death and, therefore, after they had made peace with each other at their meeting in Jerusalem.[87]

Silvanus and Mark, mentioned at the end of the First Letter of Peter, are important characters in the editorial narrative of the Canonical Edition.[88] Luke had used Mark's gospel book when he researched and wrote his own gospel book, and Luke, who refers to Silvanus with his Greek form Silas, reports that Silas distributed the letter of the Apostolic Council and promoted it in public.[89] Silvanus is mentioned in 1 and 2 Thessalonians as someone who helped Paul write letters.[90] Peter uses Silvanus the same way.

It speaks to the good relationship between Peter and Paul that both use the same scribe as they produce their letters. The position of the passage at the end of the letter indicates that Peter is writing the passage with his own hand. Once again, Theophilus had access to the autograph.

In the first letter, Peter regards "Mark" as a trusted friend; he calls him his "son."[91] In his second letter, Peter expresses the desire to write a book about Jesus that captures what he wants the faithful to remember after his death.

> *I think it right, as long as I am in this body, to refresh your memory, since I know that my death will come soon, as indeed our Lord Jesus Christ has made clear to me. And I will make every effort so that after my departure you may be able at any time to recall these things. (2 Peter 1:13–15)*

According to Theophilus's editorial narrative, Peter dictated his memoirs to Mark, confirming that Mark's gospel book was the book that Luke referred to as having been written down by a servant of the word and not an eyewitness.[92] Luke's expression "servants of the word" could simply describe trained secretaries. Early documented readers of the Canonical Edition like Papias, Tertullian, Irenaeus, and Clement of Alexandria support this understanding.[93]

Second Letter of Peter references a scene on the mountain where God revealed Jesus as his son, a scene that is included in Gospel according to Mark.

> *For he received honor and glory from God the Father when*
> *that voice was conveyed to him by the Majestic Glory, saying,*
> *"This is my Son, my Beloved, with whom I am well pleased."*
> *We ourselves heard this voice come from heaven, while we*
> *were with him on the holy mountain. (1 Peter 1:17–18)*
>
> *Then a cloud overshadowed them, and from the cloud*
> *there came a voice, "This is my Son, the Beloved; listen to*
> *him!" (Mark 9:7)*

Peter himself had "heard this voice come from heaven." And Mark wrote it down.

In Second Letter of Peter, Peter admits misunderstandings between his followers and Paul's followers, "which the ignorant and unstable twist to their own destruction." But Peter was confident that what he wrote in his letters shared the same message Paul wrote about "in all his letters."[94] Second Letter of Peter backs up Luke's harmonizing narrative that portrays Peter and Paul as colleagues and not as enemies. Theophilus demonstrates to readers of the Canonical Edition from where Luke drew his information as he wrote his book about the apostles: from Peter himself. Peter and Paul had resolved their disagreement.

The letter also includes an iconic statement about the divine origin of scripture. Although it is clearly made in the context of Jewish scriptures, it has a long history of being applied to the writings of the New Testament as well.

> *First of all you must understand this, that no prophecy of scripture is a matter of one's own interpretation, because no prophecy ever came by human will, but men and women moved by the Holy Spirit spoke from God. (2 Peter 1:20–21)*

On the background of edited collections of documents, it is a classic example of a self-endorsement. Paul does the same in his testament, Second Letter to Timothy.[95]

Letter of Jude

Jude introduces himself as the brother of James.[96] The Canonical Edition only has one list of brothers that includes James and Jude, the list of Jesus's brothers.[97] And when the brothers of Jesus are mentioned as a group in Acts and in 1 Corinthians, Jude is included.[98]

Jude writes that some intruders "pervert the grace of our God into licentiousness," addressing a point of contention between Paul's Letter to Romans and Letter of James, whether the grace of God requires good works or not. By placing the letter next to the letters of James and Peter, Theophilus expresses the opinion that Jude's blunt attacks on anonymous opponents are not to be understood as dismissing Paul.[99] Paul agrees with Jude and James that the proper interpretation of the grace of God demands an ethical lifestyle.[100]

The doxology at the end not only concludes the Letter of Jude but also brings Theophilus's Praxapostolos volume of the New Testament to a liturgically appropriate end.

> *Now to him who is able to keep you from falling, and to make you stand without blemish in the presence of his glory with rejoicing, to the only God our Savior, through Jesus Christ our Lord, be glory, majesty, power, and authority, before all time and now and forever. Amen. (Jude 24–25)*

Arrangement of Praxapostolos Volume
The arrangement of the letters is inspired by the list of the pillars of the
Jerusalem congregation in Paul's Letter to Galatians.[101]

Four Additional Letters of Paul

When it comes to the Fourteen-Letters-of-Paul volume, Theophilus
and his editors never speak with their own voices. A comparison of
the Marcionite Edition with the Canonical Edition, however, indicates
that the canonical editors renamed "Letter to Laodiceans" to "Letter to
Ephesians" and rearranged and heavily interpolated the Marcionite letter collection. These changes significantly altered the editorial narrative.

Unfortunately, the text of the Marcionite Edition is not as well
attested for the letters of Paul as it is for the gospel book, and therefore the interpolations cannot be recognized with the same accuracy. A
comprehensive interpretation of the identified interpolations has not
yet been conducted. It would certainly change the perception of the
discipline about the letters of Paul and discredit traditional approaches,
which assume that some letters were transmitted in the form that Paul
had written them.

Luckily, however, the four letters that the canonical editors added
can easily be identified, and their study might leave important clues
about the identity and agenda of the historical publisher of the Canonical Edition. These letters are Letter to Hebrews, First and Second Letters to Timothy, and Letter to Titus.

Letter to Hebrews
Letter to Hebrews opens with a statement supporting one of the goals
of the historical publisher, to show that the prophecies of Jewish scriptures are fulfilled in Jesus.

> *Long ago God spoke to our ancestors in many and various*
> *ways by the* prophets, *but in these last days he has spoken to*

us by a Son, *whom he appointed heir of all things,* through whom *he also* created the worlds. *(Hebrews 1:1–2)*

The Christological narrative and the insistence that the Creator of the universe is the divine Father of Christ fits the second-century promoters of the Canonical Edition. Next to the homily in 1 John and the editorial comments in the Gospel according to John, Letter to Hebrews is an important window into the theological beliefs of those who put the Canonical Edition together.

In typical fashion, Theophilus signals to readers that he had been able to use the original that still showed Paul's autographic subscription.[102]

> *I appeal to you, brothers and sisters, bear with my word of exhortation, for* I have written to you briefly. *I want you to know that our brother Timothy has been set free; and if he comes in time, he will be with me when I see you. Greet all your leaders and all the saints.* Those from Italy send you greetings. *Grace be with all of you. (Heb 13:22–25)*

There can be no doubt that Paul is writing these lines, as Letter to Hebrews is part of Theophilus's Fourteen-Letters-of-Paul volume. And there can also be little doubt that this subscription is a covering note to a "word of exhortation" that someone else wrote because Paul apologized for having written "to you briefly."[103] After Letter to Romans, Letter to Hebrews is the longest letter included in the Fourteen-Letters-of-Paul volume. Obviously, Paul only added a cover note.

This raises the question of who wrote this homily. Like with Mark, Luke, James, and Jude, Theophilus expects readers to identify the author, a confidant of Paul, within the context of the Canonical Edition. Paul's handwritten note, "Those from Italy send you greetings," offers the decisive clue: Paul is in Italy.[104] In his last letter, the Second Letter to Timothy, Paul wrote from Rome, "Luke is the only one with me."[105] The author of the homily that Paul sends to his friends from Rome, therefore, must be Luke.[106] Theophilus included Letter to Hebrews in his Fourteen-Letters-of-Paul volume because it preserved the subscription in the hand of Paul.

First Letter to Timothy

The Letters to Timothy and Titus share numerous features concerning style and content. The similarities function in the same way as twin forgeries: One fictitious document authenticates the other one, and by doing so, they create credibility for both documents.

According to the editorial narrative of the Canonical Edition, First Letter to Timothy is written after Paul had to leave Ephesus; he is in a hurry on his way to Macedonia and from there to Corinth. He leaves Timothy in charge of the congregation in Ephesus. This situation gives Paul the opportunity to write down the rules for good church governance.

Edited collections of documents often try to regulate communal life. The Gospel of Mary addresses one of the governance issues in second-century churches that is also addressed in First Letter to Timothy, the role of women in a congregation. Using the voice of Paul, the second-century historical publisher makes clear where he stands in the debate.

> *Let a woman learn in silence with full submission. I permit no woman to teach or to have authority over a man; she is to keep silent. (1 Timothy 2:11–12)*

It has long been observed that the infamous passage in First Letter to Corinthians, asking women to be silent in church, interrupts the context and, if removed, would not be missed by readers. This passage is a prime candidate for an interpolation by the canonical editors.[107]

Second Letter to Timothy

Second Letter to Timothy is Paul's testament, written from prison in Rome.[108] It contains a strong endorsement of Jewish scriptures, which in the history of interpretation is often applied to the writings of the New Testament as well.

> *All scripture is inspired by God and is useful for teaching, for reproof, for correction, and for training in righteousness, so that everyone who belongs to God may be proficient, equipped for every good work. (2 Tim 3:16–17)*

The letter ends with a long list of personal names and geographical locations that connect the Fourteen-Letters-of-Paul volume with Acts of Apostles and through the names of Mark and Luke to the Four-Gospel volume.

> *Demas, in love with this present world, has deserted me and gone to Thessalonica;* Crescens *has gone to Galatia, Titus to Dalmatia. Only Luke is with me. Get Mark and bring him with you, for he is useful in my ministry. I have sent Tychicus to Ephesus. When you come, bring the cloak that I left with* Carpus *at Troas, also the books, and above all the parchments. Alexander the coppersmith did me great harm; the Lord will pay him back for his deeds. You also must beware of him, for he strongly opposed our message. (. . .) Greet Prisca and Aquila, and the household of Onesiphorus. Erastus remained in Corinth; Trophimus I left ill in Miletus. (2 Tim 4:10–15, 19–20)*

Of the thirteen names, two are unique: Crescens and Carpus, who may refer to Bishop Polycarp of Smyrna and his scribe Crescens, a possible clue (or a red herring) to identify the potential historical editors and publishers of the Canonical Edition. And except for Dalmatia, all locations mentioned are familiar to readers of the Canonical Edition.[109] Dalmatia, however, is synonymous with Illyricum, which is mentioned in the interpolation at the end of Letter to Romans as the furthest reach of Paul's ministry.[110] To clandestinely add a link to the historical publisher and create a cross-link between an additional letter and an editorial interpolation is what could be expected if they all come from the same hand.

Letter to Titus

Titus, an uncircumcised Christian, was with Paul during his second visit to Jerusalem. His presence created some disagreement.[111] Paul used him as an envoy during his fundraising efforts in Macedonia. Titus's trips back and forth are well documented in the Second Letter to Corinthians.[112]

Titus was left behind on the island of Crete, where according to Acts of Apostles, Paul stopped when he was taken as a prisoner from Jerusalem to Rome.[113] Because the Marcionite Edition does not report Paul's trip from Corinth to Jerusalem and from there to Rome, this remark plays a crucial role in supporting Acts's narrative against the Marcionite Edition.

At the time of Paul's death, Titus is in Dalmatia, the furthest outpost of Paul's missionary activities.

Arrangement of Fourteen-Letters-of-Paul Volume

The Marcionite Edition arranged the letters chronologically. The conflict that drives the plot of the editorial narrative is the clash between Peter and Paul in Galatia, so the letter to Galatians is the first letter of the collection; the two letters to Corinthians cover an escalation of the battle with the Jerusalem leadership, endangering the success of Paul's fundraising effort; they cover Paul's travel from Ephesus via Macedonia and Athens to Corinth; the letter to Romans and the two letters to Thessalonians were written during Paul's stay in Corinth; Laodiceans, Colossians, Philippians, and Philemon were written from prison in Rome.

The canonical editors rearranged the letters of Paul, and they renamed the Letter to Laodiceans of the Marcionite Edition, calling it Letter to Ephesians. They broke up the chronological order and separated the letters written to congregations from the letters written to individuals. Within these sections, they arranged them according to their length, beginning with the longest letter, Letter to Romans, and ending with the shortest letter, Second Letter to Thessalonians. Luke's Letter to Hebrews is placed at the end of the letters to congregations. Letters to Timothy and Titus follow Letter to Hebrews, and Letter to Philemon concludes the Fourteen-Letters-of-Paul volume.[114] This mechanical principle of arrangement makes it challenging for readers to follow the conflict between Peter and Paul and to understand the importance of the collection for Jerusalem. In the Canonical Edition, Paul's fundraising efforts for Jerusalem seem marginal. And this may very well have been the intended effect.

§12
Who Published the Canonical Edition?

Is Theophilus the Pseudonym of Polycarp of Smyrna?

Editors and authors of anonymous or pseudonymous writings have sometimes been identified through singular expressions and philosophical concepts found in writings they had published under their own name.

The use of the term *antichrist* is such an expression. It is found in the editorial homily of 1 John and in Polycarp's Letter to Philippians.

> For everyone who does not confess that Jesus Christ has come in the flesh is antichrist. (Polycarp to Philippians 7:1)
>   By this you know the Spirit of God: every spirit that confesses that Jesus Christ has come in the flesh is from God, and every spirit that does not confess Jesus is not from God. And this is the spirit of the antichrist, of which you have heard that it is coming; and now it is already in the world. (1 John 4:2–3)

The Canonical Edition uses the term *antichrist* only in 1 and 2 John and only in editorial passages.[115] This fulfills the criteria for a singular expression, possibly allowing the identification of Theophilus as Polycarp of Smyrna.

When it comes to the provenance of the Canonical Edition, Polycarp of Smyrna is no stranger. In his provenance narrative, Irenaeus states that the Canonical Edition of the New Testament was preserved unaltered by the churches of Asia and was brought to Rome by Polycarp in the middle of the second century.[116]

Letter of Polycarp to Philippians also shows formal parallels to 1 John. It is a cover letter to an edition of the Epistles of Ignatius, which Polycarp had edited and published. Like 1 John, Polycarp talks about autographs "in our possession," and both writings contain a lengthy homily.[117] It is in this homily that the parallel expressions and convictions about the antichrist are found. Additionally, Polycarp is remembered as a prominent opponent of Marcion, which could certainly explain the anti-Marcionite bias of the Canonical Edition.

Polycarp, however, must not be mentioned in the Canonical Edition. The main argument that the promoters of the Canonical Edition use is the argument of age. It is older than the Marcionite Edition and those other publications "fabricated" by known heretics in the second century.[118] The Canonical Edition, however, is based on Theophilus's first-century edition of autographs.

Therefore, to disguise his identity, Polycarp may have used the pseudonym Theophilus, a fictitious contemporary of Luke. In this case, the many interpolations and the sixteen writings that were added to the Marcionite Edition come from the circle of Polycarp and his editors. At least one of them is known by name. A certain Crescens assisted the bishop in preparing the Epistles of Ignatius for publication, and he was also Polycarp's secretary who wrote the letter to the Philippians.[119]

As pointed out earlier, the two men may have left a record in one of the letters they added to the Marcionite Edition: "When you come, bring the cloak that I left with Carpus at Troas, also the books, and above all the parchments."[120] Carpus may just be a reference to Poly-carp(us), and the "books and parchments" may be an attempt to pacify a reader wondering about where Theophilus got the "books and auto-graphs" he is publishing. Second Timothy is addressed to Ephesus, the same city from which Theophilus, may have received the autographs of John's writings through Gaius. Troas is not far away from Ephesus, and neither is Smyrna, and a certain Crescens is mentioned in 2 Timothy three sentences earlier.[121] The plot thickens.

In the Marcionite Edition, John is a side character. He only has two lines of direct speech: "Teacher, we saw someone casting out demons in your name. And we stopped him because he does not follow together with us" (*Ev 9:49). And he says in unison with his brother James concerning the Samaritans, "Lord, do you want us to say that fire comes down from heaven and consumes them, *as Elijah has done?*" (*Ev 9:54).[122] In Marcion's edition of Paul's letters, John is mentioned casually and only once, as Paul mentions the names of the three pillars of the Jerusalem congregation.[123] Taking a side character and making him the author of a book about Jesus, preferably an auto-graph published for the first time, is a familiar strategy in publications of the second century. It is the same strategy that led the historical publisher to choose Matthew, Mark, and Luke as authors of gospel books.

In a letter to Florinus, Irenaeus emphasizes that Polycarp knew the disciple John personally and was a publicly recognized authority on John. His edition of the Letters of Ignatius would have qualified Poly-carp to authenticate, edit, publish, and promote John's autographs.

> *I can even describe the place where the blessed* Polycarp *used to sit and discourse—his going out, too, and his coming in—his general mode of life and personal appearance, together with the discourses which he delivered to the people; also how he would speak of* his familiar intercourse with John, *and with the rest of* those who had seen the Lord; *and how he*

would call their words to remembrance. *Whatsoever things*
he had heard from them respecting the Lord, *both* with
regard to His miracles and His teaching, *Polycarp having*
thus received [information] from the eyewitnesses of the
Word of life, *would recount them all* in harmony with the
Scriptures. *(Eusebius,* Ecclesiastical History *5:20:6)*

This description of Polycarp highlights three essential elements of the
publisher's narrative of the Canonical Edition: the claim of preserving
the first-century record of eyewitnesses, John as the final critical layer
of the edition, and the concept that the tradition of "respecting the
Lord, both with regard to His miracles and His teaching" was all "in
harmony with the Scriptures," an endorsement of Jewish scriptures.[124]

If the identification of Polycarp as editor of the Johannine Writings is correct, the consequences for the historical placement of the
Canonical Edition can hardly be overstated. One would have discovered not only the editor and publisher of the five Johannine writings
but also the publisher of the interpolated version of the Marcionite
Gospel, the promoter of Gospels according to Mark and Matthew, the
publisher of Acts of Apostles, the Catholic Letters, and the interpolated and enlarged edition of the Fourteen Letters of Paul.

Is Irenaeus the Historical Publisher?

As impressive as the evidence is that links Polycarp of Smyrna to the
first publication of the Canonical Edition, on second sight, the identification of Polycarp may be intended by a later publisher who wanted
to see the bishop more as a preserver of Theophilus's first-century edition than as an editor and publisher. It is remarkable that the most
important source describing the editorial narrative of the Canonical
Edition comes from the same person who also delivered the provenance narrative, Irenaeus of Lyons.[125]

When an artifact and the provenance narrative come from the
same hand, great caution is required in the art market. In the case of

proven forgeries, all too often, both the artifact and the provenance narrative were created by the same person.[126]

Irenaeus of Lyon was instrumental in promoting the authoritative use of the Canonical Edition in the Catholic Christian movement, and therefore he may be the historical person behind the literary figure of Theophilus.

VII

IMPLICATIONS

Creative Writing

WHEN JULIAN EXPANDED the traditional edition of the Letters of Ignatius or Hanthaler interpolated the material found in the Lilienfeld monastery, they wrote lengthy documents from scratch and added them to their publication. Competing Christian books on Jesus and his apostles from the second and third centuries allowed for poetic license. Most of them are fictitious, even when their implied authors, editors, and publishers insist that they are faithful copies of documents passed on without changes.

An effective strategy used in edited collections was to create not one but two or more writings that endorsed each other. These observations suggest that some or all writings added to the Marcionite Edition were creative writing exercises and were produced to support the editorial narrative. The prime candidate of a writing that was produced to support the editorial narrative of the Canonical Edition is Luke's Acts of Apostles. It explains the selection of the eight authors of the New Testament and discredits the narrative of the Marcionite Edition that postulates an unresolved conflict between "Peter and Paul."

Peter, in Second Letter of Peter, insists that his account, Gospel according to Mark, "did not follow cleverly devised myths," but that he was an eyewitness and had heard the voice of "God the Father . . . come from heaven" when he was with Jesus "on the holy mountain."[1]

And likewise, literary Paul, in his Second Letter to Thessalonians, alerts readers to misrepresentations of the salvation story of Christ and warns them of a fictitious letter "as though from us."[2] And as proof of authenticity, he adds a handwritten subscription to his letter, providing a sample of his handwriting: this "is the way I write."[3] This sample allowed the implied publisher Theophilus to verify the authenticity of all the other letters of Paul to the satisfaction of readers who trusted him.

Warning against forgeries is a common strategy of forgers. Insisting on authenticity is a common feature of manipulated documents. Swearing that they speak the truth without being prompted is what false witnesses do. The author of Mary's fictional gospel book gives Mary the line, "Do you think that I made this up by myself or that I am lying about the savior?" And the suggestion of the narrative is that Mary is not lying. Visions are as good as historical facts.

The Synoptic Problem

Second- and third-century publications on Jesus and his apostles do not quote extensively from each other. The first three gospel books of the Canonical Edition, however, share a lot of text.

When Theophilus presented Matthew's and Mark's accounts as Luke's sources, the idea that Gospel according to Luke was an expanded edition of the second-century Marcionite gospel book became an absurd proposition. This was intentional. Matthew's and Mark's accounts show readers that the Marcionite Gospel was not the oldest book on Jesus; Theophilus could provide the sources that Luke had used.

The history of interpretation demonstrates how successful Theophilus's strategy was; the traditional critical solution since Augustine was to understand Matthew as the oldest gospel, which Mark and Luke used.[4] This consensus was gradually replaced by the two-source theory, which dominated exegetical approaches during the twentieth century and assumed that a lost Source Q was shared by Matthew and Luke as they edited Mark. Both approaches fall into the trap that the historical publisher had laid out for readers of the Canonical Edition by misdirecting their attention from the Marcionite gospel book to the gospel books of Matthew and Mark. A much more probable solution to the so-called Synoptic Problem is to understand the literal parallels as shared quotes from the Marcionite Edition.

The gospel books are not the only writings in the Canonical Edition using literary parallels to boost credibility. The second chapter of Second Letter of Peter follows Letter of Jude; the structure of Paul's Second Letter to Thessalonians follows the structure of Paul's First Letter to Thessalonians; Paul's Letter to Colossians parallels Paul's Letter to Ephesians; and Letter to Titus shares style and content with the two Letters to Timothy. In each of these cases, the reader's judgment about the authenticity of one writing will carry over to the other writing, and they will become more like twins than just children of the same father. The recognition of literary parallels like these has led to the deconstruction of the Apostolic Constitutions and the Pseudo-Isidorian Decretals, which are now understood as interpolated and enlarged editions of earlier publications.

The survey of competing second-century publications on Jesus has demonstrated that the genre allows for poetic license, including inventing stories and teachings of Jesus to express second-century Christian convictions. The interpolators of Gospel according to Luke show no hesitation in using the voice of Jesus as they add text to the Marcionite Gospel.

Therefore, Gospel according to Matthew could very well be a creative writing exercise that tells the story from the perspective of the disciple Matthew using material provided by the Marcionite Gospel and structuring it by combining disjoint sayings of Jesus to speeches and organizing Jesus's actions as segues between his sermons. And likewise, Gospel according to Mark could tell the same story from the perspective of the secretary of Peter using the Marcionite gospel book. The odds are strongly in favor of such a theory compared to source-critical solutions like the two-source theory and its spinoffs.

John, Acts, and the Catholic Letters

Second-century publications about Jesus and his followers often present themselves as editions of long-forgotten, lost, secretly preserved, or otherwise unpublished autographs. The writings of John want to be interpreted this way: a manuscript about Jesus, a manuscript about prophecies, and several short autographs are brought to public attention for the first time. The historical second-century publisher of the Canonical Edition speaks with the voice of the fictitious first-century publisher Theophilus. This approach differs considerably from traditional approaches to interpreting John's writings.

Acts of the Apostles is first brought to public attention by Irenaeus in his refutation of Marcion in the last decades of the second century.[5] He argues that if Marcion accepted the first volume of Luke, he must also accept the authority of Luke's second volume, Acts of Apostles. The anti-Marcionite tendency of Acts cannot be overlooked. Peter and Paul are equals. The probability that the first promoter of a pseudonymous writing is connected to its author is very high. Acts is the central book of the New Testament in the sense that it controls the editorial narrative. The chances are that it was written more than a century after Paul's death to support the revisionist perspective of Irenaeus and his allies.

The Catholic Letters probably are not a collection of independent writings that grew over the period of one hundred years. It is very likely, for example, that the Letter of James and 2 Peter were produced for the sole purpose of supporting the anti-Marcionite editorial narrative of the Canonical Edition and providing context to First Letter of Peter and to the jarring Letter of Jude.

The Historicity of Paul

Historically, all we know of Paul came to us through the Marcionite Edition of his letters. No manuscript of the Marcionite Edition survived, only critical remarks from those who had seen the publication. The most important source for its reconstruction is the Canonical Edition, which absorbed its text and manipulated its message through rearrangements, interpolations, and additional writings, with the goal of replacing it.

Roughly nine out of ten letter collections published in antiquity are fictional and not written by the author they claim wrote them.[6]

And authors who published their own letters redacted them carefully. The letters of Paul in the Marcionite Edition were attached to a gospel book that had been handed down as trustworthy tradition according to literary Paul. This could be a grandiose effort of self-endorsement of the publication, the letters authenticating the gospel and the gospel authenticating the teachings of Paul, a popular feature of edited collections of documents. None of the extra-canonical first- and second-century publications on Jesus has been able to gain credibility among scholars of history. Why should the Marcionite Edition of the letters of Paul and his gospel book be different?

For reasons of methodological integrity, the debate about the historical Paul and the Jesus he portrays should be carried out in the context of the elusive Marcionite Edition. It is the oldest tangible literary source. And the Canonical Edition should be taken as what it is: the attempt to capture and preserve the message of the resurrected Christ as it was experienced by the evolving Catholic Christian communities of the outgoing second century.

• • •

According to this study, the publisher of the Canonical Edition interpolated and enlarged the Marcionite Edition and yet claimed to publish authentic first-century writings and documents.

When the Christian Bible is approached as a work of art, the distinction between history and story, between reality and imagination, is welcome, and the literary effort of authors, editors, and publishers is celebrated. Exegetical work, in my opinion, is an exercise in listening. Having spent most of my professional work studying the New Testament from a historical perspective, I found that understanding it as a publication of the second century satisfies the available historical evidence much better than understanding it in a first-century literary context. And it allows for a deeper appreciation of the human effort to capture the beliefs of the struggling Catholic Christian faith community that designed the editorial narrative for a collection of twenty-seven writings.

The strongest political impact of edited collections of documents sometimes comes long after their first publication. Isidore's Decretals of the ninth century set the stage for the Investiture Controversy of the eleventh and twelfth centuries. Rudolph IV's collection of documents provided the legal basis for the Habsburg rulers to become Emperors of the Holy Roman Empire decades after his death. Likewise, the Canonical Edition of the New Testament, which appeared during the second half of the second century, developed its full impact more than a century after its first publication, under Constantine the Great and his successors, when it was officially accepted as the founding narrative of the Catholic Church.

The Canonical Edition puts Jesus of Nazareth at the center of the universe. Even before the world was created, Jesus was present. Through his resurrection, he defied the laws of nature and promised eternal life to those who believed the story. This is the basic message of the Christian movement, both ancient and modern, expressed in one of the most widely distributed literary works ever published, the Canonical Edition of the New Testament.

NOTES

THE FOLLOWING NOTES are written for my peers teaching literature in the context of their academic institutions in the English, Jewish Studies, Islamic Studies, Christian Origins, Biblical Literature, and Comparative Religion departments. Standardized abbreviations are used. Primary sources in Greek, Hebrew, Latin, French, and German are quoted without translation.

I. This Thing Called New Testament

1 "Οὐ τὸ τὰ γενόμενα λέγειν . . . ἀλλ᾽ οἷα ἂν γένοιτο" (Aristotle, Poetics, 9) Manfred Fuhrmann, ed., *Aristoteles, Poetik: griechisch/deutsch* (Stuttgart: Reclam, 1994).

2 Cf. use of πιστεύειν in "Τὰ δὲ γενόμενα οὔπω πιστεύομεν εἶναι δυνατά, τὰ δὲ γενόμενα φανερὸν ὅτι δυνατά" (Aristotle, Poetics, 9) and "ταῦτα δὲ γέγραπται ἵνα πιστεύητε" (Jn 20:31).

II. When Was the Canonical Edition First Published?

1 This book uses the titles found in the first manuscripts. Usually, writings of the New Testament are referenced with an article, like "The Gospel of Mark." However, the manuscript tradition is quite clear that the editors of the Canonical Edition chose not to use "the" and not to use "of." With their title, "Gospel according to Mark," they acknowledge that more than one author has written about Jesus and that the Four-Gospel volume only presents a selection. Similarly, "Acts of Apostles," "Revelation of John," "Letter to Romans," "Letter of James," and all other writings do not carry an article in their titles. The defamiliarizing effect is intentional.

§1
The Manuscripts of the New Testament

2 David Trobisch, *The First Edition of the New Testament* (New York: Oxford University Press, 2000, 2011[2]).

3 For a list of fragmentary evidence from before the eighth century, Trobisch, *First Edition*, 29.

4 Exceptions are p[46], p[72], 05, 06, 032. Trobisch, *First Edition*, 30–34.

5 See Kurt Aland, Barbara Aland, Iōannēs Karavidopoulos, Bruce Metzger, Holger Strutwolf, and Universität Münster, *Novum Testamentum Graece*, 28th revised ed. (Stuttgart, Germany: Deutsche Bibelgesellschaft, 2017), Appendix 1.A, Codices Graeci, for an overview of the consensus. Because new manuscripts are still being discovered, this list is regularly updated, even between numbered editions.

6 The scholarly consensus dates Sinaiticus (01), Vaticanus (03) to the fourth century, Alexandrinus (02) and Ephraemi Rescriptus (04) to the fifth. *Novum Testamentum Graece*[28] Appendix 1, 799.

§2
Early Documented Readers

7 Judging from the fact that Justin's *First Apology* is addressed to Antoninus Pius and his adopted sons Marcus Aurelius and Lucius Verus, the composition must fall between 147 and 161. The reference in chapter 29 to a petition that was "a short time ago presented to Felix the governor in Alexandria" (Lucius Munatius Felix, 149–154) is used to narrow down the probable publication date to 155–157.

8 Ἔλεγχος καὶ ἀνατροπὴ τῆς ψευδωνύμου γνώσεως, cf. Eusebius, h.e. 5:7. Timothy is warned by Paul (1 Tim 6:20) to engage with "ἀντιθέσεις τῆς ψευδωνύμου γνώσεως."

9 For an extensive discussion of the passage, cf. Bernhard Mutschler, "Irenäus und die Evangelien. Literarische Rezeption 'des Herrn' und Anschluss an eine Vierertradition," in *Gospels and Gospel Traditions in the Second Century. Experiments in Reception* (BZNW: Beihefte zur Zeitschrift für die neutestamentliche Wissenschaft

235), ed. J. Schröter, T. Nicklas, and J. Verheyden (Berlin/Boston: De Gruyter, 2019), 217–252. Mutschler even speculates that the passage was taken from the library of the Roman congregation, "wahrscheinlich aus der römischen Gemeindebibliothek stammende Vierevangeliennotiz," 247. He heavily draws on the work of Claus J. Thornton, *Der Zeuge des Zeugen. Lukas als Historiker der Paulusreisen* (WUNT: Wissenschaftliche Untersuchungen zum Neuen Testament 56) (Tübingen: J. C. B. Mohr [Paul Siebeck], 1991).

10 Irenaeus, AdvHaer 1:27:1.

11 Kinzig, "Title of the NT" (1994).

12 Cf. index of citations, Otto Stählin, ed., *Clemens Alexandrinus*, vol. 4 (J. C. Hinrichs'sche Buchhandlung: Leipzig, Berlin: Akademie Verlag, 1936), 11–26. Reprint: Ursula Treu and Otto Stählin, *Clemens Alexandrinus. Bd. 4, Teil 1* (Berlin: Akademie-Verlag, 1980).

13 Lk 2:1; Mt 2.

14 Acts 11:28; 18:2.

15 Cf. Adolf von Harnack, "Anhang: Materialien zur Geschichte und Erklärung des alten römischen Symbols aus der christlichen Litteratur der zwei ersten Jahrhunderte," in *Bibliothek der Symbole und Glaubensregeln der alten Kirche,* ed. G. L. Hahn (Hildesheim: Olms, 1962³), 364–390.

16 The expression "κατὰ τὰς οἰκείας διαθήκας" (according to their own testaments) defines the identity of the group who "owns" the edition of the "testaments" like a household shares resources, which in turn sets the household apart from other communities. Clement suggests that the Old Testament was issued by "the will of God" and the New Testament through "the Lord." The adjectives in the phrase "old and catholic church" use the argument of age, and by insisting that there can only be one church applicable to all of humanity, Clement infers that all others are heretics.

17 Clement of Alexandria about Marcion's creator god: "From the heretics we have spoken of Marcion from Pontus who deprecates the use of worldly things because of his antipathy to their creator" (Stromata 3:4). Also 3:3; 3:17 where Clement addresses Marcion's disdain of sex.

18   "But since this man is the only one who has dared openly to muti-
     late the Scriptures, and unblushingly above all others to inveigh
     against God, I purpose specially to refute him, convicting him out
     of his own writings; and, with the help of God, I shall overthrow
     him out of those discourses of the Lord and the apostles, which
     are of authority with him, and of which he makes use. At pres-
     ent, however, I have simply been led to mention him" (Irenaeus,
     AdvHaer 1:29:4).

19   Cf. Matthias Klinghardt, *Das älteste Evangelium und die Entste-
     hung der Kanonischen Evangelien Band I Untersuchung 2*. Über-
     arbeitete und erweiterte Auflage ed. (Tübingen: Francke, 2020),
     391 fn 79. English translation: Matthias Klinghardt, *The Old-
     est Gospel and the Formation of the Canonical Gospels* (Leuven:
     Peeters, 2021), 409 fn 79.

§3
Provenance, Historical Conflict,
and the Canonical Edition

20   Linus is mentioned 2Tim 4:21.

21   See, The Pseudo-Isidorian Decretals, 65 ff.

22   See, Letters of Ignatius, 62 ff.

23   See, Privilegium Maius, 66 ff.

24   See, Marcionite Edition, 53 ff.

25   Because of the discrepancies in the Four-Gospel volume, we
     cannot say with certainty in what year Jesus died, making the
     often-repeated year 144 of Marcion's excommunication from the
     Roman congregation questionable. It is based on Tertullian's cal-
     culation of 115 years and 6 months from *Christ*, which in the
     tradition of interpretation is often assumed as the year 30 CE.
     "There is no doubt that he is a heretic of the Antonine period,
     impious under the pious. Now, from Tiberius to Antoninus Pius,
     there are about 115 years and 6.5 months. Just such an interval
     do they place between Christ and Marcion" (Tertullian, AdvMarc
     1:19). The only information this text communicates is that Ter-
     tullian was told that Marcion published under Antoninus Pius
     (138–161). This date corroborates Justin's claim, who dedicates

his First Apology to Emperor Antoninus, "Marcion, a man of Pontus, *who is even at this day alive,* and teaching his disciples to believe in some other god greater than the Creator" (1Apol 26). A cryptic message about letters, written by Marcion when he was a member of the Roman congregation, is referenced in AdvMarc 1:1:5 (*fidem nobiscum fuisse, ipsius litteris testibus*), and may be Tertullian's source. In my opinion, in the context of the debate between Marcionite and Canonical Edition raging during the second century in Rome, where at least one of the two parties introduced autographs of dubious origin, not much weight can be placed on such letters.

26 Eusebius, h.e. 5:13, quoting a certain Rhodo from Asia, confirms the Pontic origin of the Marcionite movement. He also reports that it was remarkably diverse, associated with different teachers who sometimes distanced themselves from Marcion, and that they disagreed even on the most essential statements about God. This is quite a different picture of the Marcionite movement from what Justin, Irenaeus, Clement of Alexandria, and Tertullian project in their writings.

27 Eusebius, h.e. 5:24:9–11.

28 Irenaeus's letter to Bishop Victor is quoted by Eusebius, h.e. 5:24:12–17.

29 "Δεῦτε ἀριστήσατε" (Jn 21:12–13).

30 Anicetus was bishop from 154/155 to 166, but the date of Polycarp's death is a matter of debate. The consensus advocates 155/156 with a strong minority vote for 166/167 and an occasional opinion for 177. Eusebius's witness seems to support the later date, but the tradition that he died at age eighty-six (MartPol 9:3) and that he was a disciple of John the Disciple of Jesus, speaks for the earlier date. Cf. Boudewijn Dehandschutter, "The Martyrium Polycarpi. A Century of Research," in *Aufstieg und Niedergang der römischen Welt,* part 2, vol. 27, 1, hg. von H. Temporini und W. Haase (Berlin: De Gruyter, 1992), 485–522, 497–503.

31 "1. In the first place, concerning the celebration of Easter Sunday: That it be observed by us on one day and at one time in all the earth, and that you should send out letters to all, as is the custom." C. Munier, *Concilia Galliae* (Turnhout: Brepols, 1963), 9.

32 Jonathan J. Armstrong, "The Paschal Controversy and the Emergence of the Fourfold Gospel Canon," in *Papers presented at the Fifteenth International Conference on Patristic Studies* held in Oxford 2007, hg. von J. R. Baun (Leuven: Peeters, 2010), 115–123.

III. What Did Competing Publications Look Like?

1 Bart D. Ehrman, *Lost Scriptures: Books That Did Not Make It into the New Testament* (Oxford: Oxford University Press, 2003), a popular translation of Early Christian publications, contains seventeen gospel books, five books of acts, thirteen epistles, and seven books of revelations. For lost works quoted by Early Christian writers, see for example the index in Stählin, *Clemens Alexandrinus*, 27–28. Willis Barnstone and Marvin Meyer, *The Gnostic Bible*, published text from forty-eight books that fit the general genre, twenty of which are not in Ehrman's collection, documenting that the genre is well and alive from antiquity to medieval times. Willis Barnstone and Marvin Meyer, eds., *The Gnostic Bible*, Revised ed. (Boston: Shambhala, 2011). Marvin Meyer, ed., *The Gnostic Gospels of Jesus: The Definitive Collection of Mystical Gospels and Secret Books about Jesus of Nazareth* (San Francisco: Harper, 2005).

2 The focus on "knowledge," Greek "gnosis," is a common feature. I am hesitant to use the term *Gnosticism* in this study because it is often used to distinguish the orthodox Christian movement from heresies of the time. I do not find this helpful. The conviction that something happened in heaven, revealed only to a select number of believers, is a central feature of the developing Catholic movement as well. What separated them from other Christian groups are details of the narrative: the God of Creation is the God of Israel, and he had only one offspring who was sent as the Son of God (Jesus), being an important distinction. Irenaeus's *Against Heresies* and Tertullian's *Against Marcion* are dedicated to the question of Catholic identity within the Christian Gnostic movement that claimed divine revelations of secrets through the spiritual experience of Christ. In my opinion, Catholic Christianity is a movement within Gnosticism.

§4
Diverse Examples

3 The Secret Book of John is preserved in four copies, NHC II, 1; III, 1; IV, 1; BG 8502, 2. It is dated to the second century because Irenaeus, *Against Heresies* 1.29, narrates part of the storyline, but he does not give the title of his source.

4 NHC II, 1:9; Marvin W. Meyer and James M. Robinson, *The Nag Hammadi Scriptures* (HarperCollins e-Books, 2014), 114, accessed January 3, 2023, http://rbdigital.oneclickdigital.com.

5 Plato's concept is expressed in the dialogue *Timaeus*. Plato distinguishes between the perfect Divinity who gave humans an eternal soul and lesser gods who crafted mortal bodies. Plato does not restrict the term *demiurge* to the lesser gods. The perfect God is called ὁ δημιουργὸς (Timaeus 28a) and ποιητὴς καὶ πατήρ τοῦ παντός (Timaeus 28c).

6 NHC III, 2; IV, 2.

7 Irenaeus, *Against Heresies* 3:11:9, mentions that the Valentinians possess a work called the *Gospel of Truth*. The third tractate of Nag Hammadi Codex I begins with those words, which provides an argument to date this book to the second century. Cf. Meyer and Robinson, *The Nag Hammadi Scriptures*, 31.

8 "In their hearts the living book of the living was revealed" parallels the concept of the Dialogue of the Savior, NHC III, 5:131–132, knowledge is stored in the heart.

9 It is thought to have been translated from a second-century Greek source. The translations are taken from Meyer and Robinson, *The Nag Hammadi Scriptures*.

10 Although missing in the only existing witness of the prescript, the conjecture "James" is certain, as the name is repeated several times in the text.

11 Cf. Justin Martyr's generic description of the canonical gospels as "memoirs of the apostles" (Justin, 1Apol 66).

12 The insistence on a miraculous discovery is a common strategy to create the impression of authenticity when documents were published for the first time, cf. Wolfgang Speyer, *Die literarische Fälschung im heidnischen und christlichen Altertum: ein Versuch ihrer Deutung* (München: C.H. Beck'sche Verlagsbuchhandlung, 1981), 44–84.

13 The Coptic version of the Gospel of Mary (Berlin Gnostic Codex 8502 = BG 8502) misses six pages at the beginning and four pages in the middle. Quotes refer to the pages in this manuscript. The text is also known from two Greek fragments (Papyrus Oxyrhynchus 3525 and Papyrus Rylands 463). It is usually dated to the second century, cf. Meyer, *Gnostic Gospels*, 36.

14 Matthew is one of the three disciples close to Jesus in the Dialogue of the Savior. On the love of Jesus for Mary, see the Gospel of Mary 10; the Gospel of Philip 59; 63–64; Pistis Sophia 17; 19. In Papyrus Rylands 463, only Levi goes out to preach.

15 Papyrus Rylands 463.

16 The Canonical Edition addresses the same conflict with the voice of Paul. On the one hand, literary Paul endorses the role of women in the community like Chloe and Phoebe. On the other hand, the Paul of the Canonical Edition insists that women should neither teach (1 Tim 2:12) nor speak at congregational meetings (1 Cor 14:34), clearly siding with Peter and Andrew against Levi in the Gospel of Mary.

17 For someone who reads a book about Jesus, the provenance of this record is not a trivial matter. Neither is it for the publisher of such a book. The answer given here is that readers will know in their hearts that this text is authentic and true.

18 Ehrman translated the edition of Émile de Strycker, *La Forme la plus ancienne du Protévangelium de Jacques* (Brussels: Société des Bollandistes, 1961). Origen references a book of James in his commentary of Gospel according to Matthew, "But some say, basing it on a tradition in the Gospel according to Peter, as it is entitled, or The Book of James, that the brethren of Jesus were sons of Joseph by a former wife, whom he married before Mary" (Origen, Comm. in Matth. 10:17). Clement of Alexandria recounts specific details of James's story concerning Mary, "For some say that, after she brought forth, she was found, when examined, to be a virgin" (Stromata 7:16). So, interpreters often conclude that "it must have been in circulation soon after 150 CE" (Ehrman, *Lost Scriptures*, 63).

19 "When Herod died, . . . Joseph got up, took the child and his mother, and went away" (Matt 2:19–23).

20 "Herod . . . killed all the children in and around Bethlehem who were two years old or under" (Matt 2:16). "For as soon as I (Elizabeth) heard the sound of your greeting, the child in my womb (John) leaped for joy" (Luke 2:44).

21 "An angel of the Lord appeared to Joseph in a dream and said, 'Get up, take the child and his mother, and flee to Egypt, and remain there until I tell you; for Herod is about to search for the child, to destroy him'" (Matt 2:13).

22 "When Joseph awoke from sleep, he did as the angel of the Lord commanded him; he took her as his wife but had no marital relations with her [καὶ οὐκ ἐγίνωσκεν αὐτὴν] until she had borne a son; and he named him Jesus" (Matt 1:24–25). The story implies that Joseph and Mary had sex after Jesus was born. According to the editorial narrative of the Canonical Edition, Jesus had four brothers and at least two sisters. "Is not this the carpenter, the son of Mary and brother of James and Joses and Judas and Simon, and are not his sisters here with us?" (Mark 6:3). "Is not this the carpenter's son? Is not his mother called Mary? And are not his brothers James and Joseph and Simon and Judas? And are not all his sisters with us?" (Matt 13:55–56). According to the editorial narrative of the Canonical Edition, the Letters of James and Jude were written by Jesus's brothers.

23 The title "Tales of the Israelite Philosopher Thomas Concerning the Childhood Activities of the Lord" (Ehrman, *Lost Scriptures*, 58) is found in a late Greek manuscript. Cf. Constantin von Tischendorf, *Evangelia Apocrypha* (Hildesheim: Georg Olms, 1987; original: Leipzig, 1867). "*Die Einleitung der Schrift (KThom 1), in der Thomas als Verfasser genannt ist, gehört nicht dazu. Die Verbindung mit diesem Namen ist also eine spätere Entwicklung, ursprünglich lautete der Titel wohl die 'Kindheitstaten Christi' oder ähnlich.*" Judith Hartenstein, "*Kindheitsevangelium nach Thomas* (KThom)" (2012) in: *WiBiLex: Das wissenschaftliche Bibellexikon im Internet* (https://www.bibelwissenschaft.de /stichwort/51906/, accessed December 9, 2022).

24 Irenaeus, AdvHaer 1:20:1. The argument cannot carry much weight, as it is possible that a later writer intentionally used the title of a lost book referenced in literature.

25 A similar and more elaborate story is told a few chapters earlier (InfThomas 6–7), where Jesus's teacher Zacchaeus says, "I was struggling to have a student, and I have been found to have a teacher" (InfThomas 7:2; Ehrman, *Lost Scriptures*, 59).

26 Additional material is underlined, missing material is marked strikethrough.

27 The Canonical Edition shares this interest and provides two accounts of Jesus's birth, one in Gospel according to Matthew and one in Gospel according to Luke. They agree on the names of Jesus's parents Joseph and Mary, and the place of Jesus's birth, Bethlehem. Almost everything else, however, is different.

28 A scholarly reconstruction of the text of the Marcionite Gospel is offered by M. Klinghardt, *Das älteste Evangelium* (2020) = *The Oldest Gospel* (English translation and revision, 2021), and for Paul's letters by Ulrich B. Schmid, *Marcion und sein Apostolos: Rekonstruktion und historische Einordnung der marcionitischen Paulusbriefausgabe* (Berlin: De Gruyter, 1995). Both works provide extensive bibliographies.

29 "I am astonished that you are so quickly deserting the one who called you in the grace of Christ and are turning to a different gospel—not that there is another gospel, but there are some who are confusing you and want to pervert the gospel of Christ. But even if we or an angel from heaven should proclaim to you a gospel contrary to what we proclaimed to you, let that one be accursed! As we have said before, so now I repeat, if anyone proclaims to you a gospel contrary to what you received, let that one be accursed!" (Gal 1:6–9). Cf. Schmid, *Marcion*, appendix I/315. Tertullian read the passage in the Marcionite Edition without noting variants to the text of the Canonical Edition. Tertullian, AdvMarc 5:2:5–6.

30 Quotes follow Klinghardt, *Oldest Gospel* (2021), volume 2, appendix 2. *Italics* indicate obscure attestation; { } indicate words "omitted by the Lukan redaction" (Klinghardt, II, 1283).

31 Nazara is mentioned *Ev 4:34; 4:16. Nazorean *Ev 24:19.

32 *Ev 4:22b (Joseph); 8:20–21 (mother and brothers).

33 *Ev 4:31; 4:23; 5:14; 7:1; 10:15. Tertullian interpreted the first sentence of this gospel book, "Jesus went down to Capharnaum, a city in Galilee" in the sense that Jesus came down from heaven:

"In the fifteenth year of the reign of Tiberius (for such is Marcion's proposition) he 'came down to the Galilean city of Capernaum,' of course meaning from the heaven of the Creator, to which he had previously descended from his own" (Tertullian, AdvMarc 4:7:1).

34 *Ev 22:1; 22:7.

35 *Ev 23:54.

36 "Now I would remind you, brothers and sisters, of the good news [=the gospel book, referenced by its title "Gospel"] that I proclaimed to you, which you in turn received, in which also you stand, through which also you are being saved, if you hold firmly to the message that I proclaimed to you—unless you have come to believe in vain. For I handed on to you as of first importance what I in turn had received: that Christ died for our sins in accordance with the scriptures, and that he was buried, and that he was raised on the third day in accordance with the scriptures, and that he appeared to Cephas, then to the twelve" (1 Corinthians 15:1–5). The passage is attested to have been included in the Marcionite Edition, but not the exact wording. Possible text differences to the Canonical Edition are not documented, cf. Schmid, *Marcion*, 325–326.

37 Schmid, *Marcion*, 286–289.

38 The editorial narrative presents letters from two settings: Gal Cor Rom 1.2Thess are written from Corinth; Laod, Col, Phil, Phm are written from Rome. For a narrative critical analysis, cf. David Trobisch, *War Paulus verheiratet?: und andere offene Fragen der Paulusexegese* (Gütersloh: Gütersloher Verlagshaus, 2011), 49–58.

39 From a literary perspective, Paul had access to writers who could help him with editing, including but not limited to Titus, Timothy, Silvanus, and Luke. It is not unusual that authors are the first publishers of their letters in antiquity. Examples: Cicero, Pliny the Younger, Seneca. Cf. David Trobisch, *Die Entstehung der Paulusbriefsammlung: Studien zu den Anfängen christlicher Publizistik* (Freiburg, Schweiz: Universitätsverlag, 1989). As all letters were written either in Corinth or Rome, readers receive a reasonable explanation in the text: Paul has time; he spends the winter in Corinth as planned (1Cor 16:5–6), and in Rome he

waited for his day in court. Kinzig, "Title of the NT" (1994), suggested that the Marcionite Edition carried the editorial title "New Testament." From a literary perspective, this is an elegant solution, because Paul declared that God (ὃς καὶ ἱκάνωσεν ἡμᾶς διακόνους καινῆς διαθήκης) made Paul and his associates servants of the New Testament (2Cor 3:6).

40 Readers of the Marcionite Edition would reconstruct Paul's trip from Damascus to Jerusalem, Antioch, Ephesus, Macedonia, Corinth, and from there directly to Rome. Cf. Trobisch, *War Paulus verheiratet?*, 74–92.

41 Tertullian, AdvMarc 5:11:4, discusses the passage without noting text differences between the Marcionite and the Canonical Edition. Cf. Schmid, *Marcion*, 328.

IV. Why Is the Canonical Edition a Collection of Autographs?

§6
Diverse Examples

1 The following summary is based on Dieter Hagedorn, *Der Hiobkommentar des Arianers Julian* (Berlin: Walter de Gruyter, 1973), XXXVII–LVII.

2 Clement, the implied publisher of the collection, is identified at the end of the collection, "The end of the Constitutions of the Holy Apostles by Clement, which are the Catholic doctrine" (ApostConst 8:47).

3 For traditional material contained in book 7, cf. Wilhelm Bousset, *Eine jüdische Gebetssammlung im siebenten Buch der apostolischen Konstitutionen* (Berlin: Nachrichten der K. Gesellschaft der Wissenschaften zu Göttingen. Philologisch-historische Klasse, 1916).

4 Greek text cf. Theodor von Zahn, *Geschichte des neutestamentlichen Kanons. 2. Urkunden und Belege zum ersten und dritten Band* (Hildesheim: Olms, 1975), 193. Revelation of John is missing in the list. For the use of δημοσιεύειν ἐπὶ πάντων (translated as "publishing for everyone") see canon 60 (ApostConst 8:47) where the expression is applied to the public reading of spurious books (ψευδεπίγραφα βιβλία) before the church.

5 For a summary of the discussion see William R. Schoedel, *Die Briefe des Ignatius von Antiochien: ein Kommentar* (München: Chr. Kaiser, 1990), 23–32.

6 Berthold Altaner and Alfred Stuiber, *Patrologie: Leben, Schriften und Lehre der Kirchenväter* (Freiburg: Herder, 1993), 256. Recurring themes are the strengthening of the role of bishops in the governance of the Church, rejection of ascetic positions, and the repetition of specific dogmatic statements. However, not everyone agrees that the interpolator and editor of the spurious writings and the editor of the collection is the same person. See Hannah, "Setting of the Long Recension" and the critique by Milton P. Brown, "Notes on the Language and Style of Pseudo-Ignatius," *JBL* 83 (1964): 146–152. Methodologically the identification is based on the observation that the final form of the collection demonstrates a unifying editorial effort and is presented to the readers as a literary unit, as one work with a beginning, an end, and with structured contents. The identification and description of this edition is greatly aided by knowing some of the written sources that were used by the editors. But the argument does not entirely depend on and is not primarily interested in identifying the sources, it is based on the plausibility of the description of the final editorial concept and process.

7 Hagedorn, *Hiobkommentar*, XXIII.

8 Hagedorn, *Hiobkommentar*, XLI: An extensive comparative study revealed surprising communalities "nicht nur in den theologischen Ansichten und der dogmatischen Terminologie, sondern auch solche allgemein stilistischer Natur, und schließlich eine große Zahl charakteristischer Topoi, wie sie sich auch innerhalb der AK selbst wiederholen." XLII: "Eindeutiger aber als diese allgemein stilistischen Ähnlichkeiten . . . beweisen die übereinstimmenden Formulierungen bestimmter Topoi die Identität der beiden Autoren. Wie sich schon die Einheit der AK hauptsächlich durch die Eigenheit des Kompilators nachweisen ließ, bestimmte Gedanken in kaum veränderter Form mehrfach vorzutragen, so ist diese Eigenart auch hier das entscheidende Kriterium."

9 Discussion of date, Hagedorn, *Hiobkommentar*, LV–LVI.

10 The following summarizes the research of Horst Fuhrmann, *Einfluss und Verbreitung der pseudoisidorischen Fälschungen: von ihrem*

Auftauchen bis in die neuere Zeit (Stuttgart: Anton Hiersemann, 1974). Edition used: Migne PL. 130 (1853), and P. Hinschius (1863).

11 Anaclet I. (ca. 79–90), the predecessor of Clement (ca. 90–101) as Bishop of Rome, also issues fictitious documents included in the collection. However, he is presented as following Clement chronologically (Fuhrmann, *Einfluß*, I, 138). The writings provided a chain of documents from the first successor of St. Peter to the implied publication date of the Decretals during the first half of the eighth century. Fuhrmann, *Einfluß*, I, 138.

12 "Through considerable portions, Pseudo-Isidore did not forge his materials freely, but rather composed them of highly varied, often heavily edited excerpts. The number of these excerpts, pieced together like a mosaic, could have amounted to more than ten thousand" (Horst Fuhrmann, "Pseudo-Isidorian Forgeries," in *Papal Letters in the Early Middle Ages*, ed. Detlev Jasper and Horst Fuhrmann [Washington, DC: Catholic University of America Press, 2001], 135–195).

13 Fuhrmann, "Pseudo-Isidorian Forgeries," 143. Horst Fuhrmann, "The Pseudo-Isidorian Forgeries," in *Papal Letters in the Early Middle Ages*, ed. Detlev Jasper and Horst Fuhrmann (Washington, DC: Catholic University of America Press, 2001), 135–195.

14 The term Pseudo-Isidore was probably coined by David Blondel (1628), cf. Fuhrmann, *Einfluß*, I, 137.

15 The name Isidore may reflect the beginning of the Dionysio-Hadriana (Fuhrmann, *Einfluß*, I, 180) where Saint Isidore writes about his intent to end the collection at the time of Saint Gregor (Gregor I, 590–604). This fits the dates of Isidore of Seville who died 636. However, the collection ends with the Roman Synod of Pope Gregor II. (715–731) April 5, 721 (Fuhrmann, *Einfluß*, I, 181).

16 Fuhrmann, *Einfluß*, I, 178–179: "An Quellenarten hat er verarbeitet: reichlich die Bibel, . . . Konzilsbeschlüsse, Dekretalen, römisch-rechtliche Quellen, Volksrechte, Kapitularien, Bußbücher, Schriften und Briefe von Kirchenvätern, Bischöfen und privaten Personen, das Glaubensbekenntnis Kaiser Justinians I., das Constitutum Constantini, den Liber Pontificalis, Ordensregeln." The fictitious Papal letters are mostly created from the Liber Pontificalis,

which provide the basic information used to construct documents issued by individual popes (Fuhrmann, *Einfluß*, I, 183–184).

17 "Sie wollten den Suffraganbischof dem Zugriff des jeweiligen Metropoliten entziehen und ihn vor der Provinzialsynode als Gerichtsstand und der weltlichen Gewalt sichern" (Fuhrmann, *Einfluß*, I, 223). The fictitious documents describe a situation where the papal authority decides controversial issues, a historical inaccuracy both for the suggested time of the fictitious documents as well as for the time of the first readers of the edited collection. "Die Vorstellung, dass Rom von jeher die ganze Kirche in Ost und West unmittelbar regiert habe, wird mit einer gesetzlichen Fundierung versehen. Der römische Brauch wird als überall verpflichtend hingestellt, und jener Satz, der Papst habe nie geirrt und werde auch künftig nie irren, wird ebenfalls als feste rechtliche Bestimmung aufgeführt" (Helmut Lüpke, *Historische Fälschungen als Werkzeug der Politik*. 2. Aufl ed. [Berlin: Junker u. Dünnhaupt, 1940], 13).

18 The Decretals clearly express the interests of Hinkmar's (845–882) opponents (Fuhrmann, *Einfluß*, I, 195). Hinkmar of Reims provides the first witness to the existence of the Pseudo-Isidorian Decretals.

19 Concerning the letter by Lupus of Ferrières, who conducted the inquiry with Nikolaus I, see Fuhrmann, *Einfluß*, II, 248 ff. Fuhrmann, "Pseudo-Isidorian Forgeries," 192: "To document his attitude and his decisions, Nicholas did not need to resort to forgeries, but it was precisely due to their congruence with his concepts that the Pseudo-Isidorian Decretals entered Rome not as a stranger but as a confirmation of many of the papacy's own convictions."

20 Hinkmar of Laon, the opponent of Hinkmar of Reims, was involved in the early dissemination of the Decretals. "Er hatte den Klerus seiner Diözese gezwungen, eine Sammlung pseudoisidorischen Rechts zu unterschreiben, und jeden, der die Unterschrift verweigerte, mit der Exkommunikation und gar mit dem Tode bedroht" (Fuhrmann, *Einfluß*, I, 224). However, it is not clear whether he instigated the production of these fictitious documents or whether he fell victim to those who had produced them. Matthias Flacius Illyricus was the first one to recognize the spurious nature in 1559. The argument was further developed by

the reformed preacher David Blondel in his Pseudo-Isidorus et Turrianus vapulantes (Genf, 1628). Among other observations he pointed out that some of the papal letters quoted authors who had lived centuries after the time when the letter was supposedly written. More recently Klaus Zechiel-Eckes identified manuscripts that most likely were used to produce the Decretals. Cf. Klaus Zechiel-Eckes, "Zwei Arbeitshandschriften Pseudoisidors. (Codd. St. Petersburg F. V. I. 11 und Paris lat. 11611)," *Francia* 27, no. 1 (2000): 205–210, http://dx.doi.org/10.11588 /fr.2000.1.46456. Klaus Zechiel-Eckes, "Ein Blick in Pseudoisidors Werkstatt. Studien zum Entstehungsprozess der falschen Dekretalen. Mit einem exemplarischen editorischen Anhang (Pseudo-Julius an die orientalischen Bischöfe, JK +196)," *Francia* 28, no. 1 (2001): 37–90. Klaus Zechiel-Eckes, "Auf Pseudoisidors Spur, oder: Versuch, einen dichten Schleier zu lüften," in *Fortschritt durch Fälschungen?: Ursprung, Gestalt und Wirkungen der pseudoisidorischen Fälschungen; Beiträge zum gleichnamigen Symposium an der Universität Tübingen vom 27. und 28. Juli 2001*, ed. Wilfried Hartmann and Gerhard Schmitz (Hannover: Hahn, 2002), 1–28.

21 The editorial narrative of the Pseudo-Isidorian Decretals is expressed in the selection of writings, selection of authors, and features like titles, arrangement, and editorial passages that introduce, summarize, or connect the individual writings of the collection.

22 Wilhelm Wattenbach, *Die österreichischen Freiheitsbriefe: Prüfung ihrer Echtheit und Forschungen über ihre Entstehung.* (Vienna, Austria: Archiv für Kunde österreichischer Geschichts-Quellen, 1852), Bd. 8, 19.

23 The name Privilegium maius creates a link to the Privilegium minus. The authenticity of the Privilegium minus was not doubtful. It still existed in the original at the time of Petrarch. The original has since disappeared, the oldest copy is manuscript 929, f. 146, Stiftsbibliothek Klosterneuburg, from the thirteenth century.

24 Wattenbach, *Die österreichischen Freiheitsbriefe*, 6. The text of the five documents is included in the appendix, Wattenbach, *Die österreichischen Freiheitsbriefe*, 32–43.

25 Wattenbach, *Die österreichischen Freiheitsbriefe*, 6–7.

26 Wattenbach was not able to determine which historical conflict the regulations addressed. The privilege was applied at a later point in time when Tirol was acquired (Wattenbach, *Die österreichischen Freiheitsbriefe*, 7).

27 The oldest copies also contained a confirmation of the Privilegium minus and the threat of punishment for those who did not keep its ordinances (Wattenbach, *Die österreichischen Freiheitsbriefe*, 8).

28 Wattenbach, *Die österreichischen Freiheitsbriefe*, 8. The text is printed in the appendix, Wattenbach, *Die österreichischen Freiheitsbriefe*, 42–43.

29 Rudolph gathered written endorsements from bishops and other political leaders. Petrarch's letter is dated March 21 (probably 1360), additional endorsements are dated July 11, 1360, "Er legte sie in seiner Hofburg zu Wien dem päpstlichen Nuntius, Bischof Egidius von Vicenza, dem Bischof Gotfried von Passau, und den Aebten Eberhard von Reichenau und Lampert von Gengembach vor, und diese hatten kein Bedenken, ihm am eilften Juli 1360 ein Transsumt auszufertigen" (Wattenbach, *Die österreichischen Freiheitsbriefe*, 20).

30 "Carl V. verbot ausdrücklich den Gerichten, die Originale dieser Privilegien einzufordern, 'noch disputiren oder darüber erkennen zu lassen'" (Wattenbach, *Die österreichischen Freiheitsbriefe*, 8).

31 Wattenbach, *Die österreichischen Freiheitsbriefe*, 21–26.

32 The same methodology, to concentrate on the time of the first appearance in public of the collection instead of on the time of the individual writings, was used earlier to date the Canonical Edition. The example shows that the reconstruction of a historical conflict addressed in the editorial narrative allows to date the first publication of Duke Rudolph IV's edited collection of documents to the middle of the fourteenth century, although the documents themselves insisted to have been written centuries earlier.

33 Wattenbach, *Die österreichischen Freiheitsbriefe*, 8.

34 Edited collections of autographs are often political publications. They are concerned with the well-being of the community. Leaders like bishops, superintendents, elders, apostles, or the pope endorse denominational traditions, not scholars of history.

35 M. Tangl, "Die Fälschungen Chrysostomus Hanthalers," *Mitteilungen des Instituts für Österreichische Geschichtsforschung* 19, no. 1 (1898): 1–54.

36 Chrysostomus Hanthaler, *Continens Propyleum Fastorum Sive Elogia X. Genealogico-Historica primorum Austriæ Marchionum ac Ducum Babenbergicorum, ceu Majorum Serenissimi Ducis Fundatoris Leopoldi VII. Gloriosi, ab Anno DCCCCVIII. usque MCC,* vol. 1 (Linz: Ilger, 1747).

37 "Ganz zwingend ist nur der Nachweis von Anachronismen, nicht nur von Unrichtigkeiten sondern von Unmöglichkeiten, und ihn hoffe ich in einer ganzen Reihe von Fällen zu erbringen" (Tangl, "Die Fälschungen Chrysostomus Hanthalers," 19).

38 Tangl, "Die Fälschungen Chrysostomus Hanthalers," 7. The manuscript by Pernold had disappeared from the holdings of the library where Hanthaler insisted he had used it, when Tangl looked for it (Tangl, "Die Fälschungen Chrysostomus Hanthalers," 10). Also, Hanthaler quoted a document from 1251 that had not been listed in otherwise reliable compilations of the thirteenth, fifteenth, and seventeenth centuries and that cannot be found in the present holdings (Tangl, "Die Fälschungen Chrysostomus Hanthalers," 18).

39 Tangl, "Die Fälschungen Chrysostomus Hanthalers," 10.

40 Tangl, "Die Fälschungen Chrysostomus Hanthalers," 2–3.

41 A similar process had worked for the editors of the enlarged collection of Ignatius's letters and the Pseudo-Isidorian Decretals, who added writings they had authored themselves to their collections of traditional material.

42 The following assessment is based on Tangl, "Die Fälschungen Chrysostomus Hanthalers," 24–25.

43 Tangl, "Die Fälschungen Chrysostomus Hanthalers," 25, footnote 1.

44 H. R. Trevor-Roper, *The Last Days of Hitler* (London: Pan, 2012). First published 1947. The following description of events is based on A. Sisman, *An Honourable Englishman: The Life of Hugh Trevor-Roper* (New York: Random House, 2011).

§8
Implications of Understanding the Canonical Edition as an Edited Collection of Autographs

45 "For God so loved the world that he gave his only Son, so that everyone who believes in him may not perish but may have eternal life" (John 3:16).

46 The German language distinguishes between *Verleger*, *Lektor*, and *Autor*.
47 "Isidorus Mercator servus Christi lectori conservo suo et parens in domino fidei salutem. Compellor a multis tam episcopis quam reliquis servis dei canonum sententias colligere et uno in volumine redigere et de multis unum facere. Sed hoc me oppido conturbat, quod diversae interpretationes varias sententias faciunt, et licet unus sit sensus, diversae tamen sunt sententiae, et aliae longiores, aliae breviores" (http://www.pseudoisidor.mgh.de/html/001.htm, accessed April 4, 2020).
48 The publisher's voice becomes distinguishable when it talks about the author or the editor, or when it references the finished book; the publisher always speaks from a later point in time than the author.
49 The implied publisher Isidore is selling his interpolations to the readers as if they were traditional and had happened during the process of transmitting the manuscripts and expressed different interpretations. "Although different interpretations" of the same documents had produced "variations," "there can only be one meaning."
50 David Trobisch, "The New Testament in the Light of Book Publishing in Antiquity," in *Editing the Bible: Assessing the Task Past and Present*, ed. John S. Kloppenborg, and Judith H. Newman (Atlanta: Society of Biblical Literature, 2012), 161–164.

V. The Design of the Canonical Edition

1 Acts 28:30–31.
2 According to Irenaeus's provenance narrative (AdvHaer 3:3:3), the line of custodians of the Canonical Edition begins with Linus, who is with Paul in Rome as he awaits his trial. Cf. 1Tim 4:21.

§9
Theophilus and the Writings of John

3 The distinction between publisher, editors, and author often forms part of the editorial narrative of edited collections. The *Secret Book of John*, the *Secret Book of James*, the *Infancy Gospel of*

James, Josephus's comments in his introduction to *Jewish War* and *Against Apion*, or Tertullian's introduction to *Against Marcion*, to name just a few publications available in the second century. All expect their readers to be aware of the publishing process.

4 John 21:24. They identified the author as John in the title, Gospel according to John.

5 The quote is, "Lord who is it?" and the referenced passage is Jn 13:23–25: "One of his disciples—the one whom Jesus loved—was reclining next to him; Simon Peter therefore motioned to him to ask Jesus of whom he was speaking. So, while reclining next to Jesus, he asked him, 'Lord, who is it?'"

6 For Lazarus, Jn 11:1–3 references Jn 12:1–2; for Caiaphas, Jn 18:13 references Jn 11:49–50; for Judas Iscariot, Jn 6:68–71 references Jn 18:2–3. Cf. David Trobisch, "The Gospel according to John in the Light of Marcion's Gospelbook," in *Das Neue Testament und sein Text im 2. Jahrhundert*, ed. Jan Heilmann and Matthias Klinghardt (Tübingen: Francke, 2018), 171–181.

7 (Jn 12:4–8) But Judas Iscariot, one of his disciples,* said, "Why was this perfume not sold for three hundred denarii and the money given to the poor?"** Jesus said, "Leave her alone. She bought it so that she might keep it for the day of my burial. You always have the poor with you, but you do not always have me."
  * The one who was about to betray him.
  ** He said this not because he cared about the poor but because he was a thief; he kept the common purse and used to steal what was put into it (Cf. Jn 13:27–29).

8 Apparently, the manuscript was being prepared for publication after John had died. Certainly, John had been dead for a while and Jesus had not returned when readers bought and read the Canonical Edition during the second century.

9 For a more detailed interpretation cf. Trobisch, "The Gospel according to John in the Light of Marcion's Gospelbook." D. Trobisch, "The voice of John in the Canonical Edition of the New Testament," in *The Identity of Israel's God in Christian Scripture*, ed. Festschrift Christopher Seitz (Atlanta, GA: SBL Press, 2020), 305–322.

10 Some translations (cf. NRSV) put some of these editorial asides in parenthesis; the oldest Greek manuscripts, however, have no

structural markers, they do not even indicate spaces between the words, so they do not indicate the beginning and end of an editorial comment. In the NRSV John 21:20–24 reads: Peter turned and saw the disciple whom Jesus loved following them; he was the one who had reclined next to Jesus at the supper and had said, "Lord, who is it that is going to betray you?" When Peter saw him, he said to Jesus, "Lord, what about him?" Jesus said to him, "If it is my will that he remain until I come, what is that to you? Follow me!" So the rumor spread in the community that this disciple would not die. Yet Jesus did not say to him that he would not die, but, "If it is my will that he remain until I come, what is that to you?" This is the disciple who is testifying to these things and has written them, and we know that his testimony is true.

11 They said to him, "Rabbi,* where are you staying?" He said to them, "Come and see." . . . One of the two who heard John speak and followed him was Andrew, Simon Peter's brother. He first found his brother Simon and said to him, "We have found the Messiah."** He brought Simon to Jesus, who looked at him and said, "You are Simon son of John. You are to be called Cephas"***
* Which translated means *Teacher*. ** Which is translated *Anointed*. *** Which is translated *Peter*. (Jn 1:38–42)

12 Now when Jesus learned that the Pharisees had heard, "Jesus is making and baptizing more disciples than John"* he left Judea and started back to Galilee. But he had to go through Samaria. So, he came to a Samaritan city called Sychar, near the plot of ground that Jacob had given to his son Joseph. Jacob's well was there, and Jesus, tired out by his journey, was sitting by the well. It was about noon. A Samaritan woman came to draw water, and Jesus said to her, "Give me a drink."** The Samaritan woman said to him, "How is it that you, a Jew, ask a drink of me, a woman of Samaria?"***
* Although it was not Jesus himself but his disciples who baptized. **His disciples had gone to the city to buy food. ***Jews do not share things in common with Samaritans. (Jn 4:1–9)

13 Nicodemus said to him, "How can these things be?" Jesus answered him, "Are you a teacher of Israel, and yet you do not understand these things? Very truly, I tell you,* if I talk to you

about earthly things [like the wind] and you do not believe, how can you believe if I tell you about heavenly things [like the Spirit]?"**

* We speak of what we know and testify to what we have seen; yet you do not receive our testimony.

** No one has ascended into heaven except the one who descended from heaven, the Son of Man. And just as Moses lifted up the serpent in the wilderness, so must the Son of Man be lifted up, that whoever believes in him may have eternal life. For God so loved the world that he gave his only Son, so that everyone who believes in him may not perish but may have eternal life. Indeed, God did not send the Son into the world to condemn the world, but in order that the world might be saved through him. Those who believe in him are not condemned; but those who do not believe are condemned already, because they have not believed in the name of the only Son of God. And this is the judgment, that the light has come into the world, and people loved darkness rather than light because their deeds were evil. For all who do evil hate the light and do not come to the light, so that their deeds may not be exposed. But those who do what is true come to the light, so that it may be clearly seen that their deeds have been done in God. (Jn 3:9–21)

14   Jn 1:6.

15   There was a man sent from God, whose name was John. He came as a witness to testify to the light, so that all might believe through him. He himself was not the light, but he came to testify to the light (Jn 1:6–8). Lk 3:1–22 (missing in the Marcionite Edition); Mk 1:1–11; Mt 3:1–17.

16   Jn 11:1.

17   Now as they went on their way, he entered a certain village, where a woman named Martha welcomed him into her home. She had a sister named Mary, who sat at the Lord's feet and listened to what he was saying (Lk 10:38–39).

18   Lk 7:36–38 versus Jn 12:1–3.

19   Luke 5:1–3.9–10 versus John 21:1–2.14. Cf. Trobisch, *John in the Light of Marcion*, 177–178.

20   Mk 16:7; Mt 28:16–20.

21 Acts has an account of the ascension of Jesus but changes its location and date.

22 Lk 24 versus John 20–21.

23 (Jn 5:14–20) Later Jesus found him in the temple and said to him, "See, you have been made well! Do not sin anymore, so that nothing worse happens to you." The man went away and told the Jews that it was Jesus who had made him well. Therefore, the Jews started persecuting Jesus, because he was doing such things on the sabbath. But Jesus answered them, "My Father is still working, and I also am working." *

   * For this reason, the Jews were seeking all the more to kill him, because he was not only breaking the sabbath, but was also calling God his own Father, thereby making himself equal to God. Jesus said to them, "Very truly, I tell you, the Son can do nothing on his own, but only what he sees the Father doing; for whatever the Father does, the Son does likewise. The Father loves the Son and shows him all that he himself is doing; and he will show him greater works than these, so that you will be astonished." (Jn 5:14–20)

   The editorial exposition (*) references the text by repeating the words "Jews," "Sabbath," and Jesus's expression "my father." It also provides background information from outside the text about the mindset of the Judean opposition. These formal features match the observations made with other editorial remarks.

24 *Indeed, just* **as the Father raises the dead and gives them life**, *so also the Son gives life to whomever he wishes.* **The Father judges no one but has given all judgment to the Son**, *so that all may honor the Son just as they honor the Father. Anyone who does not honor the Son does not honor the Father who sent him. Very truly, I tell you, anyone who hears my word and believes him who sent me has eternal life, and does not come under judgment, but has passed from death to life. Very truly, I tell you,* **the hour is coming**, *and is now here, when the dead will hear the voice of the Son of God, and those who hear will live. For just as the Father has life in himself, so he has granted the Son also to have life in himself; and he has given him authority to execute judgment, because he is the Son of Man. Do not be astonished at this; for the hour is coming when all who are in their graves will hear his voice and will come out—those who have*

*done good, to the resurrection of life, and those who have done evil, to the resurrection of condemnation. I can do nothing on my own. As I hear, I judge; and my judgment is just, because I seek to do not my own will but the will of him who sent me. If I testify about myself, my testimony is not true. There is another who testifies on my behalf, and I know that his testimony to me is true. **You sent messengers to John**, and he testified to the truth. Not that I accept such human testimony, but I say these things so that you may be saved. He was a burning and shining lamp, and you were willing to rejoice for a while in his light. **But I have a testimony greater than John's.** The works that the Father has given me to complete, the very works that I am doing, testify on my behalf that the Father has sent me. And the Father who sent me has himself testified on my behalf. You have never heard his voice or seen his form, and you do not have his word abiding in you, because you do not believe him whom he has sent. **You search the scriptures** because you think that in them you have eternal life; and it is they that testify on my behalf. Yet **you refuse to come to me to have life**. I do not accept glory from human beings. But I know that you do not have the love of God in you. I have come in my Father's name, and you do not accept me; if another comes in his own name, you will accept him. How can you believe when you accept glory from one another and do not seek the glory that comes from the one who alone is God? Do not think that I will accuse you before the Father; **your accuser is Moses**, on whom you have set your hope. If you believed Moses, you would believe me, for he wrote about me. But if you do not believe what he wrote, how will you believe what I say?* (Jn 5:21–47)

25 The storyline of the Gospel of Mary speaks to the conflict between what Jesus says in a vision to Mary and what the disciples heard Jesus say when he was with them.

26 In the beginning was the Word, and the Word was with God, and the Word was God. He [the Word] was in the beginning with God. All things came into being through him, and without him not one thing came into being. What has come into being in him was life, and the life was the light of all people. The light shines in the darkness, and the darkness did not overcome it. (Jn 1:1–5)

27 Like many second-century gospel books, Theophilus referenced the creation story in Genesis and elaborated on it.

28 There was a man sent from God, whose name was John. He came as a witness to testify to the light, so that all might believe through him. He himself was not the light, but he came to testify to the light. The true light, which enlightens everyone, was coming into the world. (Jn 1:6–9)

29 Examples are the Secret Book of John, the Holy Book of the Great Invisible Spirit, and the Dialogue of the Savior.

30 He was in the world, and the world came into being through him; yet the world did not know him. He came to what was his own, and his own people did not accept him. But to all who received him, who believed in his name, he gave power to become children of God, who were born, not of blood or of the will of the flesh or of the will of man, but of God.*

*(1) And the Word became flesh and lived among us, and we have seen his glory, the glory as of a father's only son, full of grace and truth. (2) John testified to him and cried out, "This was he of whom I said, 'He who comes after me ranks ahead of me because he was before me.'" (3) From his fullness we have all received, grace upon grace. The law indeed was given through Moses; grace and truth came through Jesus Christ. No one has ever seen God. It is God the only Son, who is close to the Father's heart, who has made him known. (Jn 1:10–18)

31 This is he of whom I said, "After me comes a man who ranks ahead of me because he was before me" (Jn 1:30).

32 Καὶ αὕτη ἐστὶν ἡ μαρτυρία τοῦ Ἰωάννου (Jn 1:19).

33 This is the testimony given by John when the Jews sent priests and Levites from Jerusalem to ask him, "Who are you?" He confessed and did not deny it, but confessed, "I am not the Messiah." And they asked him, "What then? Are you Elijah?" He said, "I am not." "Are you the prophet?" He answered, "No." Then they said to him, "Who are you? Let us have an answer for those who sent us. What do you say about yourself?" (Jn 1:19–22).

34 Rev 1:2 could reference the two genres combined in the manuscript of the Beloved Disciple, "testifying to the Word of God" (ὃς ἐμαρτύρησεν τὸν λόγον τοῦ θεοῦ) indicating the monologues,

"testifying to what he saw of Jesus Christ" (καὶ τὴν μαρτυρίαν Ἰησοῦ Χριστοῦ ὅσα εἶδεν) indicating the eyewitness account.

35 "The revelation of Jesus Christ, which God gave him to show his servants what must soon take place; he made it known by sending his angel to his servant John, who testified to the word of God and to the testimony of Jesus Christ, even to all that he saw. Blessed is the one who reads aloud the words of the prophecy and blessed are those who hear and who keep what is written in it; for the time is near" (Rev 1:1–3). For an introduction to the performance of literature in antiquity, Richard F. Ward and David J. Trobisch, *Bringing the Word to Life: Engaging the New Testament through Performing It* (Grand Rapids, MI: Eerdmans, 2013), 3–33.

36 Another parallel is the Spirit of Truth in the gospel. The Spirit is concerned with "things that are to come" (Jn 16:13) and nicely corresponds to Jesus Christ's revelation to John about "what must soon take place" (Rev 1:1–3). The publisher introduced John as someone "who testified to the word of God," to the "testimony of Jesus Christ," and to what "he saw." Rev 1:2, "τὴν μαρτυρίαν Ἰησοῦ Χριστοῦ ὅσα εἶδεν," literally translates as "the witness of Jesus Christ which he saw."

37 "I, John, . . . was on the island called Patmos because of the word of God and the testimony of Jesus. I was in the spirit on the Lord's Day, and I heard behind me a loud voice like a trumpet saying, 'Write in a book what you see and send it to the seven churches, to Ephesus, to Smyrna, to Pergamum, to Thyatira, to Sardis, to Philadelphia, and to Laodicea'" (Rev 1:9–11). The expression "the word of God and the testimony of Jesus" is an excellent description of the literary genre of Jesus's monologues in Gospel according to John as well.

38 Rev 1:1.

39 Example Rev 2:5–7:
[Spirit:] He said in a loud voice, "Fear God and give him glory, for the hour of his judgment has come; and worship him who made heaven and earth, the sea and the springs of water." Then another angel, a second, followed, saying, "Fallen, fallen is Babylon the great! She has made all nations drink of the wine of the wrath of her fornication." Then another angel, a third, followed them, crying with a loud voice, "Those who worship the beast

and its image, and receive a mark on his forehead or on his hand, he too will drink the wine of God's anger, poured undiluted into the cup of His wrath. The admonition of Rev 2:7 is repeated in 2:11.17.29; 3:6.13.22; 13:9."

40 Rev 13:1–10 as a script performed by different voices:
[John:]
And I saw a beast rising out of the sea, having ten horns and seven heads; and on its horns were ten diadems, and on its heads were blasphemous names. And the beast that I saw was like a leopard, its feet were like a bear's, and its mouth was like a lion's mouth. And the dragon gave it his power and his throne and great authority. One of its heads seemed to have received a death-blow, but its mortal wound had been healed.
[Spirit:]
In amazement the whole earth followed the beast. They worshiped the dragon, for he had given his authority to the beast, and they worshiped the beast, saying, "Who is like the beast, and who can fight against it?" Also it was allowed to make war on the saints and to conquer them. It was given authority over every tribe and people and language and nation, and all the inhabitants of the earth will worship it, everyone whose name has not been written from the foundation of the world in the book of life of the Lamb that was slaughtered.
[Editors:]
Let anyone who has an ear listen: If you are to be taken captive, into captivity you go; if you kill with the sword, with the sword you must be killed. Here is a call for the endurance and faith of the saints.

41 The reference to the "book" of life may have triggered the remark by those who were preparing the manuscript for publication. The interest in what was written down at "the foundation of the world," fits many second-century Jewish and Christian publications, including Gospel according to John's editorial prologue.

42 Example Rev 14:6–13:
[John:] Then I saw another angel flying in midheaven, with an eternal gospel to proclaim to those who live on the earth—to every nation and tribe and language and people.
[Spirit:] He said in a loud voice, "Fear God and give him glory, for the hour of his judgment has come; and worship him who

made heaven and earth, the sea and the springs of water." Then
another angel, a second, followed, saying, "Fallen, fallen is Babylon the great! She has made all nations drink of the wine of
the wrath of her fornication." Then another angel, a third, followed them, crying with a loud voice, "Those who worship the
beast and its image, and receive a mark on their foreheads or on
their hands, they will also drink the wine of God's wrath, poured
unmixed into the cup of his anger, and they will be tormented
with fire and sulfur in the presence of the holy angels and in the
presence of the Lamb. And the smoke of their torment goes up
for-ever and ever. There is no rest day or night for those who
worship the beast and its image and for anyone who receives the
mark of its name."
[Editors/Choir:] Here is a call for the endurance of the saints,
those who keep the commandments of God and hold fast to the
faith of Jesus.
[John:] And I heard a voice from heaven saying, "Write this:
Blessed are the dead who from now on die in the Lord."
[Spirit:] "Yes," says the Spirit, "they will rest from their labors, for
their deeds follow them."

43   Rev 22:10–17 as a script performed by different voices:
[John:]
I, John, am the one who heard and saw these things. And when
I heard and saw them, I fell down to worship at the feet of the
angel who showed them to me; but he said to me, "You must
not do that! I am a fellow servant with you and your comrades
the prophets, and with those who keep the words of this book.
Worship God!"
[Spirit:]
And he said to me, "Do not seal up the words of the prophecy of
this book, for the time is near. Let the evildoer still do evil, and
the filthy still be filthy, and the righteous still do right, and the
holy still be holy. See, I am coming soon; my reward is with me,
to repay according to everyone's work. I am the Alpha and the
Omega, the first and the last, the beginning and the end."
[Editors:]
Blessed are those who wash their robes, so that they will have
the right to the tree of life and may enter the city by the gates.

Outside are the dogs and sorcerers and fornicators and murderers and idolaters, and everyone who loves and practices falsehood.
[Spirit:]
"It is I, Jesus, who sent my angel to you with this testimony for the churches. I am the root and the descendant of David, the bright morning star."
[Editors:]
The Spirit and the bride say, "Come."
And let everyone who hears say, "Come."
And let everyone who is thirsty come. Let anyone who wishes take the water of life as a gift.

44 The implied publisher referred to this angel in the very first sentence, "he made it [revelation of Jesus Christ] known by sending his angel to his servant John" (Rev 1:1). The last sentence of the editorial introduction opens the liturgical frame: "Blessed is the one who reads aloud the words of the prophecy, and blessed are those who hear and who keep what is written in it; for the time is near" (Rev 1:3).

45 The invitation to "come and eat" with the resurrected Jesus in Jn 21:12 (δεῦτε ἀριστήσατε) and the invitation of the Spirit here to come and drink "the water of life" can easily be understood as an invitation to participate in the eucharist as part of the liturgical reading of Gospel according to John and Revelation of John.

46 The function of the sentences is the same as modern copyright declarations in publications. Trobisch, "Book Publishing in Antiquity," 162–165.

47 Rev 22:20–21 as a script performed by different voices:
[Spirit:]
The one who testifies to these things says, "Surely I am coming soon." Amen.
[Choir:]
"Come, Lord Jesus!"
[Editors:]
The grace of the Lord Jesus be with all the saints. Amen.

48 The wish of grace at the end is similar to the wish of grace at the end of most letters of Paul, again suggesting a liturgical reading of the books of the Canonical Edition, the setting that was suggested by Justin Martyr, see above 11 ff. A nice parallel in

extra-canonical gospels for liturgical responsive readings is found in the opening chapters of the Infancy Gospel of James.

49 On text-critical grounds the genre designation "letter" cannot be established with certainty, the minimalist title "First of John" however can be secured for the archetype of the manuscript tradition. Inscriptio: ΙΩΑΝΝΟΥ ΕΠΙΣΤΟΛΗ ΠΡΩΤΗ: ˹Ιωαν(ν)ου πρωτη Α Β² ¦ Ιωαννου καθολικη πρωτη επιστολη 18 ¦ - ℵ* Β* ¦ txt ℵ¹.

50 3 John 13. The corresponding verse in 2 John replaces the word "pen" (διὰ μέλανος καὶ καλάμου 3 John 13) with "paper" (διὰ χάρτου καὶ μέλανος 2 John 12), "Although I have much to write to you, I would rather not use paper and ink." This may indicate that the original of 2 John that the publisher used had been dictated to a professional scribe so it could be easier to read in public, whereas 3 John was a personal note written to a friend in the hand of the author with no intention to be published.

51 Ἔγραψά τι τῇ ἐκκλησίᾳ (3Jn 9).

52 Cf. "See how large letters I write when I write with my own hand (Ἴδετε πηλίκοις ὑμῖν γράμμασιν ἔγραψα τῇ ἐμῇ χειρί)" (Gal 6:11).

53 Cf. the similar statement for Gospel according to John, "We know that his testimony is true" (Jn 21:23).

54 The publisher's allusion to John's autographs as the word that "we have seen with our eyes, what we have looked at and touched with our hands" will not be wasted on readers who believe the publisher's claim that the Canonical Edition is based in great part on first-century autographs.

55 Prologue (1:1–10); Annotated Autograph (2:1–27). The editorial notes are: 1* 2:1b–6; 2* 2:7b; 3* 2:9–11; 4* 2:15–20; 5* 2:22–25; 6* 2:27.

56 See above, Voice of the editors, p. 83 ff. David Trobisch, "The Voice of John in the Canonical Edition," in *The Identity of Israel's God in Christian Scripture*, ed. Don Collett, Mark Elliott, Mark Gignilliat, and Ephraim Radner (Atlanta, GA: SBL Press, 2020), 305–322.

57 The editors use "the world" with a negative connotation as if it was created by the evil one. "From the beginning," "the word of God," and having "knowledge" reference the creation narrative

in Genesis, as Theophilus had done in the prologues to the Gospel and First John. "Only the human who does the will of God will receive eternal life" is common ground with the Gnostic myth of the demiurge, which tries to avoid the notion that God created the good and the evil.

58 "By this you know the Spirit of God: every spirit that confesses that Jesus Christ has come in the flesh is from God" (1 John 4:2). "No one has ever seen God; if we love one another, God lives in us, and his love is perfected in us" (1 John 4:12).

59 "ὁ ἔχων τὸν υἱὸν ἔχει τὴν ζωήν· ὁ μὴ ἔχων τὸν υἱὸν τοῦ θεοῦ τὴν ζωὴν οὐκ ἔχει" (1Jn 5:12).

60 1Jn 5:13–15. The argument that this is from the autograph is made because of the introduction "Ταῦτα ἔγραψα ὑμῖν," which parallels the other quotes. However, one would have to argue that the addressed audience will ask for "ὅτι ζωὴν ἔχετε αἰώνιον." The connection to a catch-word as was the case in the other editorial comments is missing. Alternatively, "ἔγραψα" is commonly used at the end of writings, the Aorist of letter writing expressing the very act of writing down the words. The word could simply indicate the beginning of an autographic subscription or the concluding thoughts of the author.

61 In Gospel according to John, John's manuscript comes to an end at the end of chapter 20. The publisher's epilogue (Jn 21) also features a quote from John's manuscript (Jn 21:2–23) with several editorial notes (in Jn 21:19.21.23, see Voice of the editors, p. 114) and concludes with personal remarks from the publisher, speaking first in first-person plural (Jn 21:24) and then in singular (Jn 21:25). Revelation also ends by featuring quotes from John's manuscript (including the voice of the Spirit), editorial comments, and concludes with the publisher addressing readers of the Canonical Edition (See End of the Book, p. 92). Likewise, 1 John introduces the epilogue with a final quote from John's autograph and finishes it with a note from the publisher addressing the readers of the Canonical Edition.

62 1Jn 5:20–21. From a second-century perspective, the statement reflects the Gnostic narrative: A Great Invisible Spirit sends his son into the material world to deliver a message. The son delivers the message and returns to his father. Whoever believes in this

message and acts on it will receive eternal life. In Theophilus's words, the "Son of God has come and has given us understanding so that *we may know* (δέδωκεν ἡμῖν διάνοιαν ἵνα γινώσκωμεν τὸν ἀληθινόν)" (1Jn 5:20). Gnosticism preaches redemption through knowledge.

63 For the genre see for example, Horatius's introductory letter in his edited collection of letters (Ep. 1; *Horace, Satires, Epistles and Ars Poetica,* trans. H. Rushton Fairclough. LCL [Cambridge, MA: Harvard University Press, 1929]); Cyprian's letters that introduce attached edited collections of his own letters (cf. ep. 73 introduces the attached ep. 71 and ep. 70; Hans von Soden, *Die Cyprianische Briefsammlung: Geschichte ihrer Entstehung und Überlieferung* [Leipzig: Hinrich, 1904]. [With tables.]); and Polycarp's letter to Philippians introducing the attached edited collection of Ignatius's letters, "they are appended to this letter" (PolPhil 13:2). Within the Canonical Edition the publisher used the same genre in Letter to Hebrews where Paul's autographic subscription endorses an attached homily written by someone else (Hb 13:22), and in Paul's autographic letter of recommendation for Phoebe, which serves as cover note for an attached copy of his letter to Rome.

64 Ἔγραψά τι τῇ ἐκκλησίᾳ (3Jn 9).

65 One editorial comment may have been added to the Second Letter of John. [John's autograph:] "I was overjoyed to find some of your children walking in the truth, just as we have been commanded by the Father. But now, dear lady, I ask you, not as though I were writing you a new commandment, but one we have had from the beginning, let us love one another." [Editorial comment:] "And this is love, that we walk according to his commandments; this is the commandment just as you have heard it from the beginning—you must walk in it. Many deceivers have gone out into the world, those who do not confess that Jesus Christ has come in the flesh; any such person is the deceiver and the antichrist! Be on your guard, so that you do not lose what we have worked for but may receive a full reward. Everyone who does not abide in the teaching of Christ, but goes beyond it, does not have God; whoever abides in the teaching has both the Father and the Son. Do not receive into the house or welcome anyone who comes to you and does not bring this teaching; for

to welcome is to participate in the evil deeds of such a person" (2Jn 6–11). The editorial comment is discernible by the shift to first-person plural "we walk." "This is love" references "Let us love one another" in John's text. The expression "from the beginning" is an editorial favorite used in the introductions to Gospel according to John and First Letter of John.

66 2Jn 12–13. A greeting from John's congregation follows: "The children of your elect sister send you their greetings." The greetings from the congregation, therefore, authenticate the letter for readers who would not have recognized John's handwriting but would have known the people John was staying with. This is the same strategy used at the end of Romans, where the handwriting of Tertius is authenticated through the handwriting of Paul, which the publisher assumes is not questioned. No matter whether an autograph existed or not, readers must realize that the implied publisher wants to make them believe that such an autograph existed.

67 3Jn 9–10.

68 As demonstrated in Revelation of John, the context of the Canonical Edition suggests Patmos as the place where John lives as he writes (Rev 1:9). And with 1 John firmly attached to 2 John and 3 John, and because of its function as a covering note for all writings of John, Patmos may also be the place where John had written the manuscript that Theophilus used for Gospel according to John. The argument is based on the default reading instruction for any edited collection: if a question is raised in one writing and answered in another, readers need not look for an answer outside the corpus.

69 Rom 16:23; 1Cor 1:14.

70 Acts 19:29; 20:4. Derbe is also the home of Timothy. The mention of Ephesus is significant. Gaius's character in the editorial narrative points to Ephesus as the likely address of Second and Third Letters of John.

VI. The Origin of the Canonical Edition

§10
Interpolations

1 In Klinghardt's reconstruction the Marcionite gospel book is about 13,150 words long, Gospel according to Luke about

19,480. In other words, a third of Gospel according to Luke are interpolations.

2 In Acts of Apostles, a certain Lucius of Cyrene is referred to as one of the prophets and teachers: "Now in the church at Antioch there were prophets and teachers: Barnabas, Simeon who was called Niger, Lucius of Cyrene, Manaen a member of the court of Herod the ruler, and Saul. While they were worshiping the Lord and fasting, the Holy Spirit said, 'Set apart for me Barnabas and Saul for the work to which I have called them.' Then after fasting and praying they laid their hands on them and sent them off" (Acts 13:1–3). Cf. Rom 16:21 where a certain Lucius is mentioned.

3 "Only Luke is with me" [in Rome] (2Tim 4:11).

4 Λουκᾶς ὁ ἰατρὸς ὁ ἀγαπητὸς (Colossians 4:14).

5 2Tim 4:11; Phm 24; 3John; Rom 16:23; 1Cor 1:14.

6 Acts 20–28. This trip supports the editorial narrative of the Fourteen-Letters-of-Paul volume against the Marcionite Edition. The Pastoral Letters, with their mention of Crete, fit into the narrative of Acts that assumes Paul's trip to Jerusalem and then as a prisoner to Rome.

7 2Tim 4:13.

8 Luke structured his manuscript in two parts, which he numbered in first and second "Logos." Luke's introduction to the second part conveys the organization in two parts: "In the first book (Τὸν μὲν πρῶτον λόγον), Theophilus, I wrote about all that Jesus did and taught from the beginning until the day when he was taken up to heaven, after giving instructions through the Holy Spirit to the apostles whom he had chosen (ἐποιησάμην περὶ πάντων, ὦ Θεόφιλε, ὧν ἤρξατο ὁ Ἰησοῦς ποιεῖν τε καὶ διδάσκειν, ἄχρι ἧς ἡμέρας ἐντειλάμενος τοῖς ἀποστόλοις διὰ πνεύματος ἁγίου οὓς ἐξελέξατο ἀνελήμφθη)" (Acts 1:1–2). So Luke's implicit title, which follows the editorial title of the Canonical Edition, Gospel according to Luke, is "Diegesis (narrative) about the events that unfolded among us," *in two volumes.* "Διήγησις περὶ τῶν πεπληροφορημένων ἐν ἡμῖν πραγμάτων" (Lk 1:1).

9 Plato and Aristotle distinguish between μίμησις, telling a story through the voice of a character (like on stage), and διήγησις,

telling a story with the voice of a narrator. Lk 1:1 uses the term διήγησις.

10 In the editorial introduction to 1 John, the historical publisher uses Theophilus's voice to make the same statement: the Canonical Edition is published for the benefit of the faith community, to confirm what they already believed.

11 "Ὁ Πολύκαρπος ἀπήγγελλεν πάντα σύμφωνα ταῖς γραφαῖς" (Eusebius, h.e. 5:20:6). The Marcionite Gospel is quoted using the abbreviation *Ev. The chapter and verse numbers represent the verse numbers of Gospel according to Luke. The translation follows Klinghardt's edition. The placement of the canonical interpolations is marked. Deletions by the canonical editors are placed within brackets {}.

12 {+ **Lk 1:1–2:52** +} "In the 15th year of the reign of Emperor Tiberius, {+ **Lk 3:1b-4:15** +} [4:31] {- ~~Jesus~~ -} **he** went down to Capharnaum, a city in Galilee {- ~~at the sea in the territory of Zebulon and Naphtali~~ -}. And he taught them on the Sabbath days" (*Ev 3:1a–4:31). The editors add Lk 1–2 before the first sentence of *Ev and interpolate it with 3:1b–4:15, the largest blocks of text they add to the Marcionite gospel book. *Ev 4:34 is called "Jesus of Nazareth" by an unclean spirit. Here and in the following quotes {- ... -} mark text of *Ev that were omitted by the editors of the Canonical Edition, and {+ ... +} mark interpolations quoting the NRSV translation. Klinghardt's translation of the Marcionite Gospel is used.

13 *Ev 4:16–30 with interpolations from Lk 4:16–30 marked.

14 1 Kings 17:8–16. The theme that Jesus did not heal everyone is picked up in Gospel according to John, which numbers the miracles of Jesus, and very prominently in the letters of Paul, who explains in 2Cor 12 that God did not heal him although Paul asked three times during a vision.

15 "Then he said to them, 'You are without understanding and too unwieldy to believe everything I have said to you. For {- ~~it was~~ -} **was it** necessary that the Christ suffers all this {+ **and then enter into his glory?" Then beginning with Moses and all the prophets, he interpreted to them the things about himself in all the scriptures** +}'" (*Ev 24:25–28).

16 *Ev 24:41–53.

17 Cf. "ἐν πάσαις ταῖς γραφαῖς" (Lk 14:22). "τὰς γραφάς" (Lk 24:45). The narrator speaks with Jesus's voice, reflecting the strategy used in the passages spoken with the voice of the spirit in John's gospel and John's manuscript of his revelation. It reflects a common strategy of second-century publications on Jesus; see Apocryphon of John.

18 The editors, however, in this case also use Jesus's voice to endorse the editorial narrative of the New Testament as it is expressed in John's writings and Luke's Acts of Apostles: the proclamation of Jesus's dying for the forgiveness of sins will begin in Jerusalem and spread to all nations, and that the "Spirit" promised in John's autographs will be sent and will give them "power from high" is told in Acts of Apostles. Self-endorsements are a common observation made in other edited collections. The editors here use Jesus's voice not only to endorse the scriptural prophets but also to endorse as scripture the edition that they themselves are producing.

19 "Paul, a servant of Jesus Christ, called to be an apostle, set apart for the *gospel of God,* which he *promised beforehand through his prophets in the holy scriptures,* the gospel concerning his Son, who was descended from David according to the flesh, and was declared to be *Son of God with power according to the spirit* of holiness by *resurrection from the dead*" (Rom 1:1–4a).

20 The claim that Jesus was related to King David is repeated only once more in the letters of Paul, in Second Letter to Timothy, a letter that was added to the Marcionite Edition by the canonical editors. "Remember Jesus Christ, raised from the dead, a descendant of David—that is my gospel (Μνημόνευε Ἰησοῦν Χριστὸν ἐγηγερμένον ἐκ νεκρῶν, ἐκ σπέρματος Δαυίδ, κατὰ τὸ εὐαγγέλιόν μου)" (2Tim 2:8). From a literary perspective, Paul's comment "that is my gospel" references Gospel according to Luke and opposes the Marcionite Gospel, which lacked a connection between David and Jesus. The reference "κατὰ τὸ εὐαγγέλιόν μου" quotes the structure of the gospel titles in the Canonical Edition. From a second-century perspective it proves that Gospel according to Luke is older than the Marcionite Gospel, because Paul seems to quote Luke's gospel book. Readers may conclude, as Irenaeus and Tertullian suggested, that the editors of the Marcionite Edition deleted 2Tim because it presented Jesus

as the "descendant of David." Literary Paul instructs readers "not
to occupy themselves with myths and endless genealogies that
promote speculations" (1Tim 1:4) and doing so, he acknowl-
edges an awareness of the discrepancies between the genealogies
of Mt and Lk. The editorial narrative of the Canonical Edition
proposes not to quarrel but to concentrate on what Mt, Lk, and
Paul have in common: Jesus was related to David.

21 Lk 24.

22 "Jesus Christ our Lord, through whom we have received grace
and apostleship to bring about the obedience of faith among all
the Gentiles [nations] for the sake of his name, including yourselves who are called to belong to Jesus Christ" (Rom 1:4b–6).

23 The wording of the Marcionite Edition is not attested. Schmid,
Marcion, 350.

24 "I, Paul, am writing this with my own hand: I will repay it" (Phm 19).

25 Listing three other minor characters of the canonical narrative
in the same sentence—Epaphras (Col 1:7; 4:12), Aristarchus
(Col 4:10; Acts 19:29; 20:4; 27:2), and Demas (Col 4:14; 2Tim
4:10)—ties the Praxapostolos and the Fourteen-Letters-of-Paul
volume inextricably together.

26 The text of the Marcionite Edition is not attested for the beginning of Romans and the end of Philemon.

27 Schmid, *Marcion,* 289–294.

28 Origen writes that Marcion, "who interpolated the gospels and
the Apostolic writings," cut off the doxology (Rom 16:25–27).
But not only the doxology, he deleted everything after Rom 14:24
(chapters 15 and 16). "Caput hoc [Rom 16:25–27] Marcion, a
quo scripturae evangelicae et apostolicae interpolatae sunt, de
hac epistola penitus abstulit, et non solum hoc, sed et ab eo loco,
ubi scriptum est: 'omne autem, quod non est ex fide, peccatum
est' [Rom 14:24], usque ad finem cuncta dissecuit. In aliis vero
exemplaribus, id est in his, quae non sunt a Marcione temer-
ata, hoc ipsum caput diverse positum invenimus" (OrigenRom
10:43; PG 14, 1290AB).

29 "The God of peace be with all of you. Amen" (Rom 15:33).

30 "And when I arrive, I will send any whom you approve with letters to take your gift to Jerusalem. If it seems advisable that I
should go also, they will accompany me" (1Cor 16:3–4).

The expression "if it seems advisable" in the context of the fundraiser refers to the amount raised. The Greek expression ἐὰν δὲ ἄξιον ᾖ is a euphemism; it translates literally as "if it is worth it."

31 The letters of Paul in the Marcionite Edition are arranged: Written from Corinth: Gal 1.2Cor Rom 1.2Thess; written from Rome: Laod Col Phil Phm. See above, Letters of Paul, 108 ff.

32 Rom 1:11–15.

33 Acts 21–24.

34 Acts 21:17–26.

35 "Lucius" is the Latin form of Greek "Λουκᾶς," cf. Lucius in Acts 13:1. Erastus (Acts 19:22; 2Tim 4:20) is part of a dedication inscription in the theater of Corinth from the first century which can still be seen today. It would also have been discoverable by a visitor to Corinth when the Canonical Edition was first published. "A terminus ad quem, seems to be fixed by the fact, that the stone has been moved and was used in the repairing of the pavement which took place about the middle of the second century" (Henry J. Cadbury, "Erastus of Corinth," *JBL* 50 (1931): 42–58, quote p. 46).

36 At the beginning of Letter to Romans, editors may have also inserted cross-references to the canonical gospels and the Old Testament. Cf. David J. Trobisch, "Das Neue Testament im Lichte des zweiten Jahrhunderts," in *Herkunft und Zukunft der neutestamentlichen Wissenschaft*, ed. Oda Wischmeyer, Neutestamentliche Entwürfe zur Theologie 6 (Tübingen, Basel: Francke, 2003), 119–129.

37 If the address of the cover note is Ephesus, as the text indicates in the greetings, the autograph with Paul's and Tertius's writing would have been available to Theophilus in Ephesus, where he found the autographs of John.

38 Calling the fictitious scribe who made the copy of the letter to Rome "Tertius," on a literary level is playful. The scribe is neither author nor addressee, he is a "third" party and in control of the publication process. He has the same role that Carpus and Crescens have in the production of 2 Timothy. Using a historical person, Erastus of Corinth, a first-century patron who sponsored the local theater and whose inscription in the stone floor can be seen by any visitor to Corinth to this very day, is a standard

practice for historical fiction. But to call another, otherwise unattested eyewitness "Quartus," the fourth one, is again very playful. Naming eyewitnesses, even if they are made up, creates credibility for storytellers. The same strategy is used to create credibility for the otherwise unattested additional appearance of Jesus in Galilee at the end of John, "Gathered there together were Simon Peter, Thomas called the Twin, Nathanael of Cana in Galilee, the sons of Zebedee, and two others of his disciples" (John 21:2).

39 Tertullian AdvMarc 5:19:3f. Cf. Schmid, *Marcion*, 341, 353: πρωτότοκος πάσης κτίσεως, ὅτι ἐν αὐτῷ ἐκτίσθη τὰ πάντα ἐν τοῖς οὐρανοῖς καὶ ἐπὶ τῆς γῆς, τὰ ὁρατὰ καὶ τὰ ἀόρατα, εἴτε θρόνοι εἴτε κυριότητες εἴτε ἀρχαὶ εἴτε ἐξουσίαι· τὰ πάντα δι' αὐτοῦ καὶ εἰς αὐτὸν ἔκτισται.

§11
Additional Writings

40 "As Jesus was walking along, he saw a man called Matthew sitting at the tax booth; and he said to him, 'Follow me.' And he got up and followed him" (Mt 9:9).

41 "Then Jesus summoned his twelve disciples. . . . These are the names of the twelve apostles: . . . Matthew the tax collector" (Mt 10:1–3).

42 "Then the disciples came and asked him, 'Why do you speak to them in parables?' He answered, 'To you it has been given to know the secrets of the kingdom of heaven, but to them it has not been given.' . . . 'Truly I tell you, many prophets and righteous people longed to see what you see, but did not see it, and to hear what you hear, but did not hear it'" (Mt 13:10–11, 17).

43 "Βίβλος γενέσεως Ἰησοῦ Χριστοῦ" (Mt 1:1).

44 Theophilus in his introduction to Gospel according to John and First John also recalls the creation narrative at the beginning of the book of Genesis, as do the interpolations of the historical publisher in Gospel according to Luke.

45 "And David was the father of Solomon by the wife of Uriah, and Solomon the father of Rehoboam" (Mt 1:6–7) versus "He was the son (as was thought) of Joseph . . . son of Nathan, son of David" (Lk 3:23–31).

46   Lk 1:5–2:52.
47   "His mother kept all these things in her heart" (Lk 2:51).
48   Mt 2:15. Joseph's side of the story is presented in Mt 1:18–2:23.
49   "After He had suffered, He also presented Himself alive to them by many convincing proofs, appearing to them during 40 days and speaking about the kingdom of God" (Acts 1:3). Appearances of Christ in Galilee are also projected by Mark (Mk 16:7) and narrated by John (Jn 21).
50   Ἀρχὴ τοῦ εὐαγγελίου Ἰησοῦ χριστοῦ (Mk 1:1).
51   2Tim 4:11; Phm 24.
52   "Barnabas wanted to take with them John called Mark. But Paul decided not to take with them one who had deserted them in Pamphylia and had not accompanied them in the work. The disagreement became so sharp that they parted company; Barnabas took Mark with him and sailed away to Cyprus" (Acts 15:37–39).
53   "Mark the cousin of Barnabas, concerning whom you have received instructions—if he comes to you, welcome him" (Col 4:10).
54   "Your sister church in Babylon, chosen together with you, sends you greetings; and so does my son Mark" (1Pt 5:13).
55   "He [Peter] went to the house of Mary, the mother of John whose other name was Mark, where many had gathered and were praying" (Acts 12:12).
56   Mk 16:7.
57   The historical editors spin the story through editorial comments (writings of John) and unmarked interpolations (Gospel according to Luke). They add the traditions of John the Baptist to the Marcionite Edition. And the term *gospel* in the introduction to Mark is something that made it into the editorial titles in the Four-Gospel volume. The absence of Peter at the beginning of Mark's account raises the possibility that the introduction is editorial and that readers were expected to recognize where Peter's account begins, as they had done in Gospel according to John. Peter does not talk about the birth of Jesus and Jesus's baptism, because he was not there. Whose voice are we listening to in the prologue to Peter's eyewitness account? According to Theophilus's editorial narrative, we are listening to Mark.
58   "Through Silvanus, whom I consider a faithful brother, I have written this short letter to encourage you and to testify that this is the true grace of God. Stand fast in it" (1Pt 5:12).

59 "I think it right, as long as I am in this body, to refresh your memory, since I know that my death will come soon, as indeed our Lord Jesus Christ has made clear to me" (1Pt 1:13–14). The sentence can be read as a covering note, attached to a copy of Mark's manuscript, authenticating it. This is consistent with Theophilus's desire to edit and publish autographs.

60 "I too decided, after investigating everything carefully from the very first, to write an orderly account" (Lk 1:3) insinuates that the competing publications were not as well researched, specifically not "the very first" (ἄνωθεν) events, and they were not presented as "orderly" (ἀκριβῶς καθεξῆς) as the manuscript that Luke submitted to Theophilus. This critique fits Mark's gospel book well, which lacks a birth narrative and clear timeline.

61 Date, Time, and John the Baptist traditions are interpolated by the canonical editors of the Marcionite Gospel: "In the 15th year of the reign of Emperor Tiberius, {+ **when Pontius Pilate was governor of Judea, and Herod was ruler of Galilee, and his brother Philip ruler of the region of Ituraea and Trachonitis, and Lysanias ruler of Abilene, during the high priesthood of Annas and Caiaphas, the word of God came to John son of Zechariah in the wilderness.** . . . Lk 3:1–4:15 +}."

62 Rom 1:1–4. The Marcionite Gospel lacks the birth story, and it seems to have been open-ended with no ascension story.

63 Just as Theophilus placed Gospel according to John after the gospel book of Luke, which it references. Publishers of edited collections "make out of many one," as Isidore Mercator described his work. Such editorial activities are to design the titles of the books, to organize them into volumes, and to arrange them within those volumes.

64 David J. Trobisch, "The Book of Acts as a Narrative Commentary on the Letters of the New Testament: A Programmatic Essay," in *Rethinking the Unity and Reception of Luke and Acts*, ed. Andrew F. Gregory and C. Kavin Rowe (Columbia: University of South Carolina Press, 2010), 119–127. Nathanael Lüke, *Über die narrative Kohärenz zwischen Apostelgeschichte und Paulusbriefen* (TANZ: Texte und Arbeiten zum Neutestamentlichen Zeitalter 62) (Tübingen: Francke, 2019).

65 The birth as well as the ascension of Jesus are interpolations to the Marcionite Gospel.

66 Acts 1:8.

67 The eleven disciples: "Peter, and John, and James, and Andrew, Philip and Thomas, Bartholomew and Matthew, James son of Alphaeus, and Simon the Zealot, and Judas son of James"; and the family of Jesus: "Mary the mother of Jesus, as well as his brothers" (Acts 1:13–14).

68 David Trobisch, "The Council of Jerusalem in Acts 15 and Paul's Letter to the Galatians," in *Theological Exegesis: Essays in Honor of Brevard S. Childs*, ed. Christopher R. Seitz and Kathryn Greene-McCreight (Grand Rapids, MI: Eerdmans, 1999), 331–338. Both, the Jerusalem Apostles and Paul, do the same number and kind of miracles: Just as Peter and John heal a lame man outside of the Jerusalem temple (Acts 3:1–10), Paul heals a lame man in Lystra (Acts 14:8–10). Peter's shadow heals the sick in Jerusalem (Acts 5:15); in Ephesus the sick are cured by touching Paul's handkerchiefs and aprons (Acts 19:12). In Jerusalem Peter casts out unclean spirits (Acts 5:16); in Ephesus Paul casts out a spirit of divination (Acts 16:18). The story of Peter healing everyone who is brought to him in Jerusalem (Acts 5:16) is paralleled by the story of Paul curing everyone who is brought to him on Malta (Acts 28:9). In Joppa Peter raises Tabitha from the dead (Acts 9:36–41), and Paul brings young Eutychus back to life in Troas (Acts 20:9–12). In Lydda Peter heals Aeneas, who was paralyzed and had been bedridden for eight years (Acts 9:33–34), while in Malta Paul cures the father of Publius, who suffered from fever and dysentery (Acts 28:8). Cf. Trobisch, "Book of Acts as a Narrative Commentary."

69 "He [Paul] lived there [in Rome] for two whole years in his own quarters, welcoming every one who visited, preaching the kingdom of God, and teaching about the Lord Jesus Christ boldly and freely" (Acts 28:30–31).

70 As fanciful as this may seem, it is important to the historical publisher to discredit the Marcionite Edition of Paul's letters by insisting that he found the older, unedited, original text.

71 "When James and Cephas and John, who were acknowledged pillars, recognized the grace that had been given to me, they gave to Barnabas and me the right hand of fellowship" (Gal 2:9). Although the "three pillars" are quoted in most manuscripts of Gal 1:9 as James, Peter, John, the manuscript tradition is not uniform: Ιακωβος και Πετρος $\mathfrak{P}^{46}$ r ¦ Πετρος και Ιακωβος D F

G 629 ar b vg^mss; Tert Ambst Pel ¦ Ιακωβος και Κηφᾶς א*B C I^vid
K L P Ψ 0278. 33 . 81 . 104 . 365 . 630 . 1175 . 1241 . 1505 .
1739 . 1881 . 2464 𝔐 vg sy co.

72 2Tim 1:17; 4:6, 11; 1Pt 5:13, 2Pt 1:14, 3:1.

73 As the history of interpretation demonstrates, the Letters of Paul,
the Catholic Letters, and canonical gospel books can be read as
seemingly unrelated writings and offer therefore a variety of pos-
sibilities to alleviate narrative discrepancies. The editorial narrative of the historical publisher suggests one out of the many ways
to read the "sources" correctly. Cf. Trobisch, *War Paulus verheiratet?* 35–36.

74 "He [Peter] motioned to them with his hand to be silent and
described for them how the Lord had brought him out of prison.
And he added, 'Tell this to James and to the believers.' Then he
left and went to another place" (Acts 12:17). Cf. Acts 15:13;
21:18.

75 1Cor 15:7; Gal 1:19, 2:9,12.

76 "Is not this the carpenter, the son of Mary and brother of James
and Joses and Judas and Simon, and are not his sisters here with
us?" (Mk 6:3). "Is not this the carpenter's son? Is not his mother
called Mary? And are not his brothers James and Joseph and
Simon and Judas?" (Mt 13:55). "Jude, a servant of Jesus Christ
and brother of James" (Jude 1:1). The editorial narrative of the
Canonical Edition, therefore, identifies James as the brother of
Jude and Jesus.

77 "Then certain individuals came down [to Antioch] from Judea
and were teaching the brothers, 'Unless you are circumcised
according to the custom of Moses, you cannot be saved.' And
after Paul and Barnabas had no small dissension and debate with
them, Paul and Barnabas and some of the others were appointed
to go up to Jerusalem to discuss this question with the apostles
and the elders" (Acts 15:1–2).

78 James: ὁρᾶτε ὅτι ἐξ ἔργων δικαιοῦται ἄνθρωπος καὶ οὐκ ἐκ
πίστεως μόνον. Paul: εἰδότες [δὲ] ὅτι οὐ δικαιοῦται ἄνθρωπος
ἐξ ἔργων νόμου ἐὰν μὴ διὰ πίστεως Ἰησοῦ Χριστοῦ.

79 James sums up the discussion and sets the tone for the letter that
is sent out after the meeting in Jerusalem (Acts 15:13).

80 It is difficult to establish why James should have written such a
letter. Like the Gospels of Matthew and Mark, it may have been

designed for the purpose to support the editorial narrative of the Canonical Edition.

81 The expression "Dispersion" is a parallel to the address of the Letter of James, "To the twelve tribes in the Dispersion." Cf. ἐκλεκτοῖς παρεπιδήμοις διασπορᾶς (1Pt 1:1) with ταῖς δώδεκα φυλαῖς ταῖς ἐν τῇ διασπορᾷ (James 1:1).

82 "This is now, beloved, the second letter I am writing to you" (2Pt 3:1).

83 "To the exiles of the Dispersion in Pontus, Galatia, Cappadocia, Asia, and Bithynia" (1Pt 1:1).

84 "James and Cephas and John" (Gal 2:9); "when Cephas came to Antioch" (2:11); "certain people came from James" (Gal 2:12).

85 Ephesus is mentioned in Acts eight times, 1Cor 15:32; 16:8; in the title of Letter to Ephesians; 1Tim 1:3; 2Tim 1:18; 4:12. Twice in Revelation of John: Rev 1:11; 2:1.

86 According to the publisher's narrative, Asia is also the home of the recipients of John's seven letters included in Revelation of John (Rev 2–3).

87 Cf. the apostolic letter of Acts 15.

88 "Through *Silvanus*, whom I consider a faithful brother, I have written this short letter to encourage you and to testify that this is the true grace of God. Stand fast in it. Your sister church in Babylon, chosen together with you, sends you greetings; and so does my *son Mark*" (1Pt 5:12–13).

89 Acts 15:22. "We have therefore sent Judas and Silas, who themselves will tell you the same things by word of mouth" 27.32.40; 16:1.

90 1Thess 1:1, 2Thess 1:1; cf. 2Cor 1:19. Despite the phrasing, the letter is written in first-person singular, leaving little doubt to the readers that they are listening to the voice of Paul. Whatever the role of Timothy or Silvanus was, it was not an authorial role.

91 Paul calls Timothy his true child, "Τιμοθέῳ γνησίῳ τέκνῳ ἐν πίστει" 1Tim 1:2; 2Tim 1:2.

92 "καθὼς παρέδοσαν ἡμῖν οἱ ἀπ' ἀρχῆς αὐτόπται καὶ ὑπηρέται γενόμενοι τοῦ λόγου" (Lk 1:2).

93 See above, Early Documented Readers, 11 ff.

94 Cf. "ὡς καὶ ἐν πάσαις ταῖς ἐπιστολαῖς λαλῶν ἐν αὐταῖς περὶ τούτων, ἐν αἷς ἐστιν δυσνόητά τινα, ἃ οἱ ἀμαθεῖς καὶ

ἀστήρικτοι στρεβλώσουσιν ὡς καὶ τὰς λοιπὰς γραφὰς πρὸς τὴν ἰδίαν αὐτῶν ἀπώλειαν" (2Pt 3:16). Interpreted as an anachronism, typical errors in edited collections, the reference to "all his letters" references the Fourteen-Letters-of-Paul volume, which includes more letters than the Marcionite Edition. And also, the comparison of Paul's letters with "all other Scriptures" fits Theophilus's agenda of promoting the value of Jewish and Apostolic Scripture. Cf. Trobisch, *First Edition*, 86–96 for a more exhaustive discussion of cross-links.

95 2Tim 3:16–17.

96 English translations distinguish between Jude and James, the brothers of Jesus, and Judas and Jacob. In the Greek text there is no distinction.

97 Mt 13:55; Mk 6:3.

98 Acts 1:14; 1Cor 9:5.

99 Paul agrees with Jude in that "wrongdoers will not inherit the kingdom of God" (1Cor 6:9). Paul uses the example of an athlete to illustrate the effort not to indulge sinful behavior: "So I do not run aimlessly, nor do I box as though beating the air; but I punish my body and enslave it, so that after proclaiming to others I myself should not be disqualified" (1Cor 9:26–27).

100 Literary Paul is aware that some misrepresent his position and try to "slander" him. He says so explicitly in his Letter to Romans. Cf. Romans 3:7–8, "But if through my falsehood God's truthfulness abounds to his glory, why am I still being condemned as a sinner? And why not say (as some people slander us by saying that we say), 'Let us do evil so that good may come?' Their condemnation is deserved!"

101 (Gal 2:9). Although the "three pillars" are quoted in most manuscripts of Gal 1:9 as James, Peter, John, the manuscript tradition is not uniform: Ιακωβος και Πετρος 𝔓⁴⁶ r ¦ Πετρος και Ιακωβος D F G 629 ar b vg^mss; Tert Ambst Pel ¦ Ιακωβος και Κηφᾶς ℵ* B C I^vid K L P Ψ 0278. 33 . 81 . 104 . 365 . 630 . 1175 . 1241 . 1505 . 1739 . 1881 . 2464 𝔐 vg sy co. 2 Tim. 1:17; 4:6.11; 1 Pet. 5:13, 2 Pet. 1:14, 3:1.

102 From a literary perspective, Letter to Hebrews was written from Rome and to an audience in Greece and Asia Minor (Hb 13:23–24). The editorial title "Hebrews" indicates an audience that Paul

was not supposed to minister to, as Peter was made the apostle to the circumcised, "ὁ γὰρ ἐνεργήσας Πέτρῳ εἰς ἀποστολὴν τῆς περιτομῆς" (Gal 2:9).

103 Many translators add "my" exhortation, but it is not part of the Greek manuscripts. The text of Hb 13:22 is "Παρακαλῶ δὲ ὑμᾶς, ἀδελφοί, ἀνέχεσθε τοῦ λόγου τῆς παρακλήσεως, καὶ γὰρ διὰ βραχέων ἐπέστειλα ὑμῖν."

104 "Ἀσπάζονται ὑμᾶς οἱ ἀπὸ τῆς Ἰταλίας" (Hb 13:24).

105 Paul and Luke in Rome: Acts 28; 2Tim 4:11.

106 Origen also suspected Luke as a candidate to write Hebrews (Eusebius, h.e. 6:25).

107 "(As in all the churches of the saints, women should be silent in the churches. For they are not permitted to speak, but should be subordinate, as the law also says. If there is anything they desire to know, let them ask their husbands at home. For it is shameful for a woman to speak in church. Or did the word of God originate with you? Or are you the only ones it has reached?)" 1Cor 14:33–36. The parenthesis in the NRSV indicates the willingness of the translators to indicate a later, un-Pauline addition. David Trobisch, *A User's Guide to the Nestle-Aland 28 Greek New Testament* (Atlanta: Society of Biblical Literature, 2013), 55–56.

108 "May the Lord grant mercy to the household of Onesiphorus, because he often refreshed me and was not ashamed of my chain; when he arrived in *Rome*, he eagerly searched for me and found me" (2Tim 1:16–17); "As for me, I am already being poured out as a libation, and *the time of my departure has come*" (4:6); "*At my first defense* no one came to my support, but all deserted me. May it not be counted against them!" (4:16).

109 The locations mentioned are Thessalonica, Galatia, Dalmatia, Ephesus, Troas, Corinth, and Miletus. Dalmatia is the only location not mentioned anywhere else in the Fourteen-Letters-of-Paul volume.

110 "For I will not venture to speak of anything except what Christ has accomplished through me to win obedience from the Gentiles, by word and deed, by the power of signs and wonders, by the power of the Spirit of God, so that from Jerusalem and as far around as *Illyricum* I have fully proclaimed the good news of Christ" (Rom 16:18–19).

111 Gal 2:1–5.

112 2Cor 2:13; 7:6–8:1.

113 "I left you behind in Crete for this reason, so that you should put in order what remained to be done, and should appoint elders in every town, as I directed you" (Titus 1:5). Acts 27.

114 The first four letters of the Marcionite Edition are arranged according to size, not chronologically: Romans, 1, 2 Corinthians, Galatians. They are followed by the shorter letters to communities, also arranged according to their size: Ephesians, Philippians, Colossians, 1, 2 Thessalonians. Letter to Hebrews is added to the letters to congregations. The letters to individuals are also arranged according to their length: 1, 2 Timothy, Titus, Philemon.

§12
Who Published the Canonical Edition?

115 The term *antichrist* is used in the New Testament 1Jn 2:18, 22 which, according to the above analysis, are in editorial sections. The mention of 2Jn 7 is also in a section that should be seen as an editorial annotation (6–11): it references the keyword "love" in the autograph and comments on it.

116 According to Irenaeus, the chain of transmission of the Canonical Edition begins with Linus (1Tim 4:21) and leads from there via Polycarp and Anicetus into the time of Irenaeus (AdvHaer 3:3:3).

117 "We are sending to you the letters of Ignatius that were sent to us by him together with any others that we have in our possession, just as you requested. They are appended to this letter" (PolPhil 13:2).

118 Cf. Tertullian, AdvMarc 4:4.

119 "I am writing these things to you via Crescens, whom I recently commended to you and now commend again, for his conduct while with us has been blameless, and I believe that it will be likewise with you. And you will consider his sister to be commended when she comes to you. Farewell in the Lord Jesus Christ in grace, you and all those with you. Amen" (Polycarp to Philippians 14). Michael W. Holmes, *The Apostolic Fathers: Greek Texts and English Translations* (Grand Rapids, MI: Baker Academic, 2007).

120 2Tim 4:13.

121 2Tim 4:10.

122 Translation follows Klinghardt, 1296. The scene is set in Samaria. In John's manuscript it is developed into the story of Jesus and the Samaritan woman (Jn 4:1–42).

123 Gal 2:7–9.

124 Eusebius uses expressions describing Irenaeus that feel like a mix of quotes from the editorial commentary to John's manuscripts of the gospel book and his revelation, and from interpolations in the Marcionite gospel book: Irenaeus "bear(s) witness before God" about Polycarp's role in transmitting the tradition of "eye-witnesses of the Word of life" and the "things he had heard from them concerning His [Jesus's] miracles and His teaching" which was "in all harmony with the Scriptures." Irenaeus "treasured them up not on paper," but in his "heart," and was "revolving these things accurately" in his mind (Eusebius, h.e. 5:20:6–7). And the singular expression "Word of Life" (παρὰ τῶν αὐτοπτῶν τῆς ζωῆς τοῦ λόγου) is paralleled in 1Jn 1:1 (τοῦ λόγου τῆς ζωῆς). Cf. Phil 2:16 λόγον ζωῆς.

125 Adv. Haer. 3:1;1; 3:3:3.

126 Sisman, *An Honourable Englishman.*

VII. Implications

1 "For we did not follow cleverly devised myths when we made known to you the power and coming of our Lord Jesus Christ, but we had been eyewitnesses of his majesty. For he received honor and glory from God the Father when that voice was conveyed to him by the Majestic Glory, saying, 'This is my Son, my Beloved, with whom I am well pleased.' We ourselves heard this voice come from heaven, while we were with him on the holy mountain" (2Pt 1:16–18).

2 "As to the coming of our Lord Jesus Christ and our being gathered together to him, we beg you, brothers and sisters, not to be quickly shaken in mind or alarmed, either by spirit or by word or by letter, as though from us to the effect that the day of the Lord is already here" (2Thess 2:1–2).

3 "I, Paul, write this greeting with my own hand. This is the mark in every letter of mine; it is the way I write" (2Thess 3:17).

4 Augustine, De Consensu evangelistarum 1:2.

5 Trobisch, "The Book of Acts as a Narrative Commentary," 119–127.

6 Trobisch, *Die Entstehung*, 141–142.

BIBLIOGRAPHY

Aland, Kurt, Barbara Aland, Iōannēs Karavidopoulos, Bruce Metzger, Holger Strutwolf, and Universität Münster. 2017. *Novum Testamentum Graece.* 28th revised ed. Stuttgart, Germany: Deutsche Bibelgesellschaft.

Altaner, Berthold, and Alfred Stuiber. 1993. *Patrologie: Leben, Schriften und Lehre der Kirchenväter.* Freiburg: Herder.

Armstrong, Jonathan J. 2010. "The Paschal Controversy and the Emergence of the Fourfold Gospel Canon." In International Conference on Patristic Studies, *Studia patristica: Ascetica, liturgica, orientalia, critica et philologica, the First Two Centuries XLV,* edited by Jane Ralls Baun, Averil Cameron, Mark Julian Edwards, and Markus Vinzent, 115–123. Leuven: Peeters.

Barnstone, Willis, and Marvin W. Meyer. 2009. *The Gnostic Bible: Expanded Edition.* Boston: Shambhala.

Blondel, David. 1628. *Pseudo Isidorus et Turrianus vapulantes seu editio et censura nova epistolarum omnium, quas urbis Romæ Præsulibus a Clemente ad Siricium etc. Isidorus Mercator supposuit, Franc. Turrianus defendere conatus est.* Geneva: Chouët.

Bousset, Wilhelm. 1916. *Eine jüdische Gebetssammlung im siebenten Buch der apostolischen Konstitutionen.* Berlin: Nachrichten der K. Gesellschaft der Wissenschaften zu Göttingen. Philologisch-historische Klasse.

Brown, Milton P. 1964. "Notes on the Language and Style of Pseudo-Ignatius." *Journal of Biblical Literature* 83 (2): 146–152.

Cadbury, Henry J. 1931. "Erastus of Corinth." *Journal of Biblical Literature* 50 (2): 42–58.

Dehandschutter, Boudewijn. 1993. "The Martyrium Polycarpi. A Century of Research." In *Aufstieg und Niedergang der römischen Welt: Geschichte und Kultur Roms im Spiegel der neueren Forschung. 2, Bd 27. Teilbd 1, 2, Bd 27. Teilbd 1,* edited by Hildegard Temporini and Wolfgang Haase, 485–522, 497–503. Berlin: De Gruyter.

Ehrman, Bart D. 2003. *Lost Scriptures: Books That Did Not Make It into the New Testament.* Oxford: Oxford University Press.

Fuhrmann, Horst. 1974. *Einfluss und Verbreitung der pseudoisidorischen Fälschungen: von ihrem Auftauchen bis in die neuere Zeit.* Stuttgart: Anton Hiersemann.

Fuhrmann, Horst. 2001. "Pseudo-Isidorian Forgeries." In *Papal Letters in the Early Middle Ages*, edited by Detlev Jasper and Horst Fuhrmann, 135–195. Washington, DC: Catholic University of America Press.

Fuhrmann, Manfred. 1994. *Aristoteles, Poetik: griechisch/deutsch.* Stuttgart: Reclam.

Hagedorn, Dieter. 1973. *Der Hiobkommentar des Arianers Julian.* Berlin: Walter de Gruyter.

Hannah, Jack W. 1960. "The Setting of the Ignatian Long Recension." *Journal of Biblical Literature* 79 (3): 221–238.

Hanthaler, Chrysostomus. 1747. *Fasti Campililienses. Tomus I., continens Propyleum Fastorum sive Elogia X. Genealogico-Historico primorum Austriæ Marchionum ac Ducum Babenbergicorum . . . ab anno DCCCCVIII. usque MCC. item seculum I. Campililii ab anno MCCI. usque MCCC. (Tom. II. continens, parte prima, seculum Christi XV., Campililii II. Parte altera, Seculum Christi XV., Campililii III. ab anno MCCCI. usque ad annum MD., etc.-Appendix apologetica sive dialogi IX. super notulas Ortilonis de Lilienfeld ex Aloldo Peklariensi . . . nunc impugnatas, etc.).* Linz: Ilger.

Harnack, Adolf von. 1962. "Anhang: Materialien zur Geschichte und Erklärung des alten römischen Symbols aus der christlichen Litteratur der zwei ersten Jahrhunderte." In *Bibliothek der Symbole und Glaubensregeln der alten Kirche. Mit einem Anhang von Dr. Adolf Harnack*, edited by August Hahn and Adolf von Harnack, 364–390. Hildesheim: Olms.

Hartenstein, Judith. 2012. "Kindheitsevangelium nach Thomas (KThom)." WiBiLex: Das wissenschaftliche Bibellexikon im Internet. https://www.bibelwissenschaft.de/stichwort/51906/.

Hinschius, Paul. 1963. *Decretales pseudo-isidorianae et capitula angilramni ad fidem librorum manuscriptorum recensuit fontes indicavit commentationem de collectione pseudo-isidori praemisit.* Aalen: Scientia Verlag.

Holmes, Michael W. 2007. *The Apostolic Fathers: Greek Texts and English Translations.* Grand Rapids, MI: Baker Academic.

Kinzig, Wolfram. 1994. "Καινὴ διαθήκη: The Title of the New Testament in the Second and Third Centuries." *The Journal of Theological Studies* 45 (2): 519–544.

Klinghardt, Matthias. 2020. *Das älteste Evangelium und die Entstehung der kanonischen Evangelien.* Tübingen: Francke.

Klinghardt, Matthias. 2021. *The Oldest Gospel and the Formation of the Canonical Gospels.* Leuven: Peeters.

Lüke, Nathanael. 2019. *Über die narrative Kohärenz zwischen Apostelgeschichte und Paulusbriefen.* Tübingen: Francke.

Lüpke, Helmut. 1940. *Historische Fälschungen als Werkzeug der Politik.* 2. Aufl ed. Berlin: Junker u. Dünnhaupt.

Meyer, Marvin. 2005. *The Gnostic Gospels of Jesus: The Definitive Collection of Mystical Gospels and Secret Books about Jesus of Nazareth.* New York: Harper One.

Meyer, Marvin W., and Willis Barnstone. 2009. *The Gnostic Bible: Expanded Edition.* Boston: Shambhala.

Meyer, Marvin W., and James M. Robinson. 2014. *The Nag Hammadi Scriptures.* HarperCollins e-Books. http://rbdigital.oneclickdigital.com.

Migne, Jacques Paul. 1853. *Isidori Mercatoris decretalium collectio = tomum claudunt Marci Valerii Probi opusculum de notis antiquis et Aevi Carolini carmina : acc. J.-P. Migne.* Paris: Migne.

Munier, Charles, and Charles de Clercq. 1963. *Concilia Galliae.* Turnhout: Typographi Brepols Editores Pontificii.

Mutschler, Bernhard. 2019. "Irenäus und die Evangelien: Literarische Rezeption 'des Herrn' und Anschluss an eine Vierertradition." In *Gospels and Gospel Traditions in the Second Century: Experiments in Reception,* edited by Jens Schröter, Tobias Nicklas, and Joseph Verheyden, 217–252. Berlin/Boston: De Gruyter.

Robinson, James M., and Marvin W. Meyer. 2014. *The Nag Hammadi Scriptures.* HarperCollins e-Books. http://rbdigital.oneclickdigital.com.

Schmid, Ulrich B. 1995. *Marcion und sein Apostolos: Rekonstruktion und historische Einordnung der marcionitischen Paulusbriefausgabe.* Berlin: De Gruyter.

Schoedel, William R. 1990. *Die Briefe des Ignatius von Antiochien: ein Kommentar.* München: Chr. Kaiser.

Sisman, Adam. 2011. *An Honourable Englishman: The Life of Hugh Trevor-Roper.* New York: Random House.

Soden, Hans von. 1904. *Die cyprianische Briefsammlung: Geschichte ihrer Entstehung und Überlieferung.* Leipzig: Hinrich.

Speyer, Wolfgang. 1981. *Die literarische Fälschung im heidnischen und christlichen Altertum: ein Versuch ihrer Deutung.* München: C.H. Beck'sche Verlagsbuchhandlung.

Stählin, Otto, and Ursula Treu. 1980. *Clemens Alexandrinus. Bd. 4, Teil 1.* Berlin: Akademie-Verlag.

Strycker, E. de. 1961. *La forme la plus ancienne du Protévangile de Jacques, recherches sur le papyrus Bodmer 5 avec une édition critique du texte grec et une traduction annotée. En appendice Les versions arméniennes traduites en latin par Hans Quecke. Publié avec le concours du Centre national belge de recherches byzantines.* Bruxelles: Société des Bollandistes.

Tangl, M. 1898. "Die Fälschungen Chrysostomus Hanthalers." *Mitteilungen des Instituts für Österreichische Geschichtsforschung* 19 (1): 1–54.

Thornton, Claus-Jürgen. 1991. *Der Zeuge des Zeugen: Lukas als Historiker der Paulusreisen.* Tübingen: J.C.B. Mohr (Paul Siebeck).

Tischendorf, Constantin von. 1987. *Evangelia apocrypha.* Hildesheim: G. Olms.

Treu, Ursula, and Otto Stählin. 1980. *Clemens Alexandrinus. Bd. 4, Teil 1.* Berlin: Akademie-Verlag.

Trevor-Roper, H. R. 2012. *The Last Days of Hitler.* London: Pan.

Trobisch, David. 1989. *Die Entstehung der Paulusbriefsammlung: Studien zu den Anfängen christlicher Publizistik.* Freiburg, Schweiz: Universitätsverlag.

Trobisch, David. 1999. "The Council of Jerusalem in Acts 15 and Paul's Letter to the Galatians." In *Theological Exegesis: Essays in Honor of Brevard S. Childs*, edited by Christopher R. Seitz and Kathryn Greene-McCreight, 331–338. Grand Rapids, MI: Eerdmans.

Trobisch, David. 2003. "Das Neue Testament im Lichte des zweiten Jahrhunderts." In *Herkunft und Zukunft der neutestamentlichen Wissenschaft*, edited by Oda Wischmeyer, 119–129. Tübingen: Francke.

Trobisch, David. 2010. "The Book of Acts as a Narrative Commentary on the Letters of the New Testament: A Programmatic Essay." In *Rethinking the Unity and Reception of Luke and Acts*, edited by Andrew Gregory and C. Kavin Rowe, 119–127. Columbia: University of South Carolina Press.

Trobisch, David. 2011. *War Paulus verheiratet?: und andere offene Fragen der Paulusexegese.* Gütersloh: Gütersloher Verlagshaus.

Trobisch, David. 2012a. "The New Testament in the Light of Book Publishing in Antiquity." In *Editing the Bible: Assessing the Task Past and Present,* edited by John S. Kloppenborg and Judith H. Newman, 161–164. Atlanta: Society of Biblical Literature.

Trobisch, David. 2012b. *The First Edition of the New Testament.* Oxford: Oxford University Press.

Trobisch, David. 2013. *A User's Guide to the Nestle-Aland 28 Greek New Testament.* Atlanta: Society of Biblical Literature.

Trobisch, David. 2018. "The Gospel according to John in the Light of Marcion's Gospelbook." In *Das Neue Testament und sein Text im 2. Jahrhundert,* edited by Jan Heilmann and Matthias Klinghardt, 171–181. Tübingen: Francke.

Trobisch, David. 2020. "The Voice of John in the Canonical Edition of the New Testament." In *The Identity of Israel's God in Christian Scripture: Essays in Honor of Christopher R. Seitz,* edited by Donald Collett, Mark R. Elliott, Mark S. Gignilliat, and Ephraim Radner, 305–322. Atlanta: Society of Biblical Literature.

Ward, Richard F., and David Trobisch. 2013. *Bringing the Word to Life: Engaging the New Testament through Performing It.* Grand Rapids, MI: Eerdmans.

Wattenbach, Wilhelm. 1852. *Die österreichischen Freiheitsbriefe: Prüfung ihrer Echtheit und Forschungen über ihre Entstehung.* Vienna, Austria: Archiv für Kunde österreichischer Geschichts-Quellen. Bd. 8.

Zahn, Theodor von. 1975. *Geschichte des neutestamentlichen Kanons. 2. Urkunden und Belege zum ersten und dritten Band.* Hildesheim: Olms.

Zechiel-Eckes, Klaus. 2001. "Zwei Arbeitshandschriften Pseudoisidors (Codd. St. Petersburg F.v.I. 11 und Paris lat. 11611)." *Francia* 27 (1): 205–210. http://dx.doi.org/10.11588/fr.2000.1.46456.

Zechiel-Eckes, Klaus. 2002a. "Auf Pseudoisidors Spur, oder: Versuch, einen dichten Schleier zu lüften." In *Fortschritt durch Fälschungen?:*

Ursprung, Gestalt und Wirkungen der pseudoisidorischen Fälschungen; Beiträge zum gleichnamigen Symposium an der Universität Tübingen vom 27. und 28. Juli 2001, edited by Wilfried Hartmann and Gerhard Schmitz, 1–28. Hannover: Hahn.

Zechiel-Eckes, Klaus. 2002b. "Ein Blick in Pseudoisidors Werkstatt Studien zum Entstehungsprozess der falschen Dekretalen." *Francia* 28 (1): 37–90. https://doi.org/10.11588/fr.2001.1.46229.

SOURCES INDEX

16:5–6, 153
16:8, 186

2 Corinthians
1:19, 186
2:13, 189
3:6, 154
7:6–8:1, 189

Galatians
1:6–9, 152
1:19, 185
2:1–5, 189
2:7–9, 190
2:9, 12, 184, 185, 186, 188
2:11, 186
2:12, 186
2:16, 122

Philippians
2:16, 190

Colossians
1:7, 179
1:13–18, 113
4:10, 179, 182
4:12, 179
4:14, 176, 179

Hebrews
1:1–2, 127
13:22, 174, 188
13:22–25, 127
13:23–24, 187
13:24, 188

1 Thessalonians
1:1, 186

2 Thessalonians
1:1, 186
2:1–2, 190
3:17, 191

1 Timothy
1:2, 186
1:3, 186
1:4, 179
2:11–12, 128
2:12, 150
4:16, 188
4:21, 161, 189
6:20, 144

2 Timothy
1:2, 186
1:16–17, 188
1:17, 185
1:18, 186
2:8, 178
3:16–17, 129, 187
4:6, 11, 185
4:6, 188
4:10, 179, 190
4:10–15, 19–20, 129
4:11, 176, 182, 188
4:12, 186
4:13, 176, 190
4:16, 188
4:20, 180
4:21, 146

Titus
1:5, 189

Philemon
19, 179